The Garden at Night

Burnout and Breakdown in the Teaching Life

Mary Rose O'Reilley

HEINEMANN
Portsmouth, NH

Heinemann
A division of Reed Elsevier Inc.
361 Hanover Street
Portsmouth, NH 03801–3912
www.heinemann.com

Offices and agents throughout the world

The author and publisher wish to thank those who have generously given
permission to reprint borrowed material:

"A Cushion for Your Head" from *The Gift: Poems by Hafiz* translated by
Daniel Ladinsky. Copyright © 1999 by Daniel Ladinsky. Reprinted by
permission of the author.

Library of Congress Cataloging-in-Publication Data
O'Reilley, Mary Rose.
  The garden at night : burnout and breakdown in the teaching life /
Mary Rose O'Reilley.
    p. cm.
  Includes bibliographical references.
  ISBN 0-325-00848-5 (alk. paper)
  1. Teachers—Job stress. 2. Burnout (Psychology). 3. Teachers—Attitudes.
I. Title.
LB2840.2.O77 2005
371.1'001'9—dc22
                                                              2005010949

Editor: Lisa Luedeke
Production: Elizabeth Valway
Cover design: Joni Doherty
Cover photograph: Collection of the Mercer Museum of
  the Bucks County Historical Society
Composition: Argosy
Manufacturing: Louise Richardson

Printed in the United States of America on acid-free paper
09 08 07 06 05 VP 1 2 3 4 5

This book is affectionately dedicated to Robert K. Miller, whose friendship sustains me and whose rhetoric of gentleness guides me to work more skillfully in the world

Contents

Foreword

When Mary Rose O'Reilley publishes a new book, I expect three things that have made her one of my favorite writers: poetic prose that is a pure pleasure to read; fidelity to her own experience, even when it reveals her wrinkles; and dollops, even wallops, of humor, the kind that makes hard truth palatable and brings cosmic topics down to human scale. But I expect more than a good, honest read and lots of laughs from Mary Rose's writing. I expect to come away with a sense of hope about myself, my fellow travelers, and life's possibilities, the hope one gets not from being analyzed and advised but from being befriended.

The Garden at Night fulfills all of my expectations and more. And that is a wonder, because this book takes on a grim topic: the burnout and breakdown that emerge from the shadow side of the workplace. We spend half our waking lives at work, but too many of us live half-lives while we are there. We so easily get trapped in pathological patterns of thinking, relating, and acting, patterns that mirror the impersonal logic of institutions more than the imperatives of the human heart. When these deformations go unacknowledged and unchecked, burnout and breakdown are nearly inevitable—bringing suffering not only to those who do the work but to those whom the work is meant to serve. Becoming a burned-out teacher or physician is not a fate to be desired, but neither is being taught by the one nor treated by the other.

In *The Garden at Night*, Mary Rose O'Reilley resists the temptation to blame these pathologies solely on the conditions of the workplace, as tempting and morally convenient as it is to do so. Instead, she challenges us to take personal responsibility for the way we collaborate in creating disheartening environments and invites us on an inner journey toward taking heart in our work once again. More than that, she offers disciplines for the inner journey, so seamlessly woven into her meditations that she avoids sounding as if she is writing an owner's manual for the soul.

I keep referring to "the workplace," even though *The Garden at Night* is aimed specifically at "burnout and breakdown in the teaching life." Teachers will indeed find special insight here, insight not generally available in the literature on teaching. Where other than in this book can teachers get help in reflecting on "softening our relationship to time" or "mourning and prophetic witness in school"? Topics such as these open up teaching and learning as the profoundly spiritual enterprise it is and encourage us to start sounding its depths.

But I persist in pointing to the workplace at large because this book is written at a depth of soul that makes its insights applicable to people in any of life's roles. Mary Rose O'Reilley writes here about the work she knows best. But I cannot imagine a workplace where her wisdom would not illumine and enliven those who labor in it. Indeed, I cannot imagine a person who would not find guidance in what Mary Rose says for all the far reaches of being alive, well beyond the work we do and the places where we do it.

So get ready to find your own experience of work named, reframed, and illumined as you read, laugh, and reflect your way through the pages that lie ahead. But above all, get ready to experience a transformative way of looking at the workplace, the people you work with, and yourself in the midst of it all.

Parker J. Palmer

Prologue: Contemplative Pedagogy

This book is about living, as a teacher, what the spiritual traditions call a contemplative vocation. I'll begin by raising some questions that will go to the heart of our journey together. Contemplative pedagogy, in my mind, has to do with focused attention, silence, hospitality, and humility, and so my questions generally have to do with our experience of these ways of being.

What kind of attention do you, the teacher, pay? What is the relationship between the quality of your attention and your need to control the situation? (If we are really listening, we cannot control things very well, and yet "classroom order" is one of the things teachers are most likely to be evaluated on.)

What is the place of silence in your classroom? What kinds of silence do you invite? When and how? Do you distinguish between good silence and bad silence? How do you know the difference?

Are you able to regard your texts—be they of physics or poetry—as products of spiritual life and spiritual search? If you perceive the materials of your discipline this way, what difference does it make to the life of the classroom? We teach students how to analyze, *otherize*, anatomize—this kind of instruction is not inherently wrong, in fact, it is central to our western cultural agenda; I think it is exactly 50 percent useful—but how can we design a classroom that values connection and wholeness, where one spiritual presence interpenetrates another, be it of student and student, student and teacher, student and text? What would have to change?

I've been thinking a lot since September 11, 2001, about the Buddhist idea of "first thoughts." The goal of meditation, in this tradition, is to bring us gracefully into the present moment. The discipline of "sitting" tends to erase our hard drive, if you will, and leads us to see (as Christian writers also recommended) "all things new." By contrast, ordinary thinking is mostly thoughts about thoughts—a rehashing of the newspaper, our own tedious ruminations, traditional drills, mom's injunctions. We've had a few years, now, of thoughts about thoughts on 9-11. Pundit culture quickly imposed a series of cant phrases on this event, as it does on any crisis, for this is how human beings make history and understand their lives. But such repetitions can become instruments of authoritarian control, each phrase a hammer blow that bangs another bar in place and creates the formidable cage of received opinion. Since much academic communication is *thought about thought*, how can we get ourselves, our disciplines, and our students to retain a hidden freshness? How can we preserve a space for something more like *first thoughts*? First thoughts are dangerous to express because they inevitably challenge control of the cultural story, a story that people cling to because it serves them very well.

If you are willing to allow that your students might have a rich and authoritative inner life, how do you nourish it rather than negate it? How do you "receive the guest as Christ"—to use the Benedictine formulation, realizing, as the Benedictine Sister Joan Chittister has written, that the stranger is the only one who might be able to teach us something new (1990, 125)?

Implicit in these questions is what may seem, in the midst of our hectic schedules, an odd query: *where is our down time?* People learn a lot when they are resting and not performing. How can we get this contemplative space into the classroom? To reemphasize my earlier point, what happens if the teacher doesn't control everything that happens? How can we get ourselves to pay attention, rather than constantly planning and calculating, and make the class come out where we want it? How much can we quiet down?

When I began teaching college English in 1967, I started by trying to define for myself a pedagogy of nonviolence. We were at the height of the Vietnam War, and my course was one of those introductory ones used to wash out students who then became vulnerable to the draft. Teachers of that generation had to make connections quickly between what they were doing in the classroom and the authoritarian structures outside it. Were there ways in which traditional teaching methods made students more likely to become the playthings of force? That was my question. What enables us to resist, I concluded, are certain habits of being: one has to have an inner life and be familiar with its contours; one has to know how to bring the inner world into dialogue with the terrain of other minds, traditions, and teachers; having entered upon that rather unstable and shifting ground, we require strategies for nonviolent conflict resolution because disagreements will break out. We will inevitably be challenged to take on intellectual and emotional tasks that are almost beyond the capacity of anyone trained in the western tradition. In the crucible of that encounter, we will have a chance to develop courage and confidence and practical strategies.

I thought that if I could create a classroom situation that worked according to those principles, my students might still enlist in the army, but at least they would do so with intentionality and presence, not as mindless sheep.

I have been teaching a long time now, and a review is in order: how effective were these strategies, either in the human community or as the foundation of an academic life? As to the first, I cannot judge. It is only my own life in the academy that I can comment on.

I'm still here—and dare I say, in these troubled times?—still having fun.

Let me make a quick transition to a recent week. As I was getting my syllabus in order for a new course on T. S. Eliot and Virginia Woolf, I was asking myself: what can I put in place that will help these students, first, become conscious of their own inner worlds and how different they might be from Eliot's or Woolf's, or different from mine or the students in their circle? Second, how can I help them become conscious and analytical about the water they are swimming in, as fish in an ocean of postmodern, post–9-11 data? Finally, how can I help them use that analytical position as a perspective from which to view the concerns of the Modernists? I resolve to set up classroom experiences that will nourish these emotional and intellectual perspectives, and if I succeed, my students will not enlist in the army, or, if they do, they will not do so as mindless sheep.

Has anything changed?

Superficially, no. In the intervening years since 1967 and today, however, one of the things I've been doing in my spare time is raising sheep, working part-time on a local farm. I have discovered that sheep can outsmart me almost every time.

From the outside, nothing much has changed in my classroom since 1967; but many things have changed in my inner world. Back then, I was angry a lot of the time, as well as a perfectionistic and *driven* individual. Now I am more likely to look at my syllabus and think, like Garfield the cat, "Where can we fit a nap in here?"—because I now know that much of what happens in the classroom happens when we are, at some level, napping. When I developed what I framed as a pedagogy of nonviolence, I tried to decenter the classroom, putting the chairs in a circle and refusing to be the center of authority and control. My students and I journalled together, wrote personal responses to our texts, questioned—also, I might add, we did a lot of analytical writing and *answering* of questions. Most of the teachers of my generation, led by Ken Macrorie and Peter Elbow, were pursuing similar experiments. It was no big deal.

But between the day I put the chairs in a circle and the day I got tenure, all hell broke loose. Those new pedagogies made people—administrators, tenure committees—antagonistic. The German theologian Dorothee Soelle has written, "A language that takes our emotions seriously and gives them real weight in our lives encourages us to think and be and act differently" (1984, 84). Administrators and many of my colleagues—and, on bad days, I myself—do not really want to hear from a student thinking and being and acting differently.

Why was I surprised?

I was naïve and young. I began with the idea that we in the academy would love to hear from independent thinkers who believe their personal experience to be important. Yet, psychologists like Alice Miller, who has argued so passionately for what came to be called *expressivist pedagogies,* has specifically tied these classroom arrangements to a certain quality of *defiance*: "Our capacity to resist has nothing to do with our intelligence but with the degree of access to our true self" (1985, 43). I found out that not only do most administrators and parents not want to deal with a young person so engaged, but also students themselves quickly catch on that it might not be in their own interests to access the inner world. Then they will have to face the bother and inconvenience of resisting whatever insults the soul. Then they will suffer. What I did not take into account when I wrote my earlier books was *suffering.* To be stretched almost beyond where you can go is acutely painful. One often fails—as teacher, as student—and failure brings more pain. One must court doubt and despair in the process of learning anything at all. That is why the analytical framework I have chosen for this book, forbidding as it might seem, is what the sixteenth-century Christian mystic John of the Cross called the *dark night of the soul.*

The trouble and controversy that quickly gathered around my modest attempts at defining a pedagogy of nonviolence put me on a spiritual journey. The models we have for struggle—faithfulness to vision, the contempt of our communities and rotten salary—are spiritual ones. And what enables us to survive the pratfalls of this path are spiritual disciplines: humility, abandonment, a compassionate heart, and a hermeneutics of silence. About 1972 I was writing that it seemed impossible to teach English, at least in the overstimulated way I had adopted, without also teaching some form of meditation. In the face of boredom, burnout, and breakdown, I found John of the Cross more practical than John Dewey. Later I undertook a Buddhist apprenticeship, in Thich Nhat Hanh's monastery, Plum Village, where I learned to sit without a goal but simply with a practice. I learned that every difficulty that arises is your dearest teacher. Simultaneously, I was studying spiritual direction in a Christian context at Shalem Institute for Spiritual Formation in Bethesda, Maryland—an odd series of postdoctoral choices, I'm sure anyone will agree, undertaken to help me grapple with the pain of my choices.

Contemplation is a radical exercise. Since finishing the program at Shalem, I have been doing spiritual direction, or spiritual companioning, as I prefer to call it, with young ministers and clergy people. Typically, we begin with ten minutes or so of chitchat, settle down to twenty minutes of silence, then talk for another half hour or so. After a few months of this, my young ministers often leave the church. This is kind of a joke to my housemates, who watch the ministers come and go, taking off their white plastic collars on the way out.

"What do you *say* to them?"

"Nothing."

One archetypal young assistant pastor visited with me last year.

"How was your day?" I'd ask.

On one of his days that stands out in my recollection, he told me he'd prayed over the body of a woman who had been torn apart in an elevator accident; then he had visited with a family in mourning after a murder. One of the brothers of the deceased chased him off with a rifle. Then he went home to his suburban church and listened to three women fighting over the placement of the Christmas wreath.

We sat in silence for twenty minutes, and then he went home. A few weeks later, he told me he was going to start a business doing decoupage and faux painting.

I don't do much for my spiritual direction clients. They arrive at my house in much the same frame of mind that I go to the swimming pool after teaching all day. The pool doesn't talk to me, but it changes everything. Thich Nhat Hanh taught us this *gatta*, a little formulaic prayer: "Breathing in I become still water, calmly reflecting." Calm reflection is the *radix* of contemplative practice. In a literature classroom, silence makes us face the consequences of our texts. Usually we'd rather not face these consequences, which is why we assign so many. The underlying message of many syllabi is, *whatever you do, don't read these books*; or, if you manage to turn the pages, don't think about them. English majors are always confessing to me after graduation, while they are working as telephone solicitors and so on, how much fun it is to read the books they pretended to read in college.

Allow some space and silence in your classroom and watch how everything changes—everything is up for grabs, your whole life. If you really look at your day, the dislocations become apparent. Fortunately, in this quiet space, you can also learn what you need to do to survive. That's why my young ministers so often leave the Christmas wreath hanging and enter the quieter trades. Very often, they become teachers.

Acknowledgments

A book is beholden to all kinds of people who influence its direction, often more productively than its author. To those who gave me assignments as a visiting speaker and invited me into collegial conversations, I'm particularly grateful: above all to the faculty and administration at Berea College, Berea, Kentucky. Libby Jones deserves special thanks.

Mike Heller of Roanoke College in Virginia invited me to write what evolved into the essay "Nobody in This Lifeboat Looks Like Leonardo DiCaprio." David Laurence of MLA and his staff further shaped the direction of that piece when it came out in *ADE*. Lad Tobin, Bruce Ballenger, and I originally tossed around the ideas in "Practicing the Koans of Professional Life" at CCCCs. "The Mystic, the Prophet, and the Rhetorician" evolved from a CCCCs panel with Mike Heller and Paul Puccio. The most profound conversations that resonate in this book occurred in classrooms, among students. I would like to thank especially the students in "The Contemplative Practice of Writing Nature," Nate Schultz in particular.

For much of the theoretical frame that informs my analysis of John of the Cross, I'm indebted to my teachers and colleagues at Shalem Institute for Spiritual Formation, Bethesda, Maryland, especially to Constance Fitzgerald and Gerald May. Its dialogue with Buddhism originated in my study with Thich Nhat Hanh at Plum Village.

My colleagues at the University of St. Thomas, especially Michael Mikolajczak, chair of the English department, and my dear friend Bob Miller, put up with more than anyone should have to keep this book on track; Bob's editorial acuity contributed, yet again, whatever nuance a work of mine may possess.

Generous grants from the University of St. Thomas, the Minnesota State Arts Board, the McKnight Foundation, and the American Council of Learned Societies gave me the necessary reassigned time to write.

My sister, Margaret Plumbo, M.S., a certified nurse-midwife and faculty member at the University of Minnesota, contributed not only her unfailing support but keen professional insight as well—as did my grown children, Jude and Julian O'Reilley.

Whatever I write is indebted to friends who have led and counseled me my whole professional life, especially Peter Crysdale, Peter Elbow, Paul Lacey, and Parker Palmer; at the same time, the work and brave examples of young colleagues like Laura Milner fill me with hope. Finally, I'm grateful to Lisa Luedeke at Heinemann for taking the journey of this book with me. Thank you.

Chapter 1

Practicing the
Koans of Professional Life

Breakdown and Breakout

So: I'm going to begin by writing about burnout and break-down in professional life. I will look at this unfashionable topic in light of two traditional frames: first, the Buddhist notion of koan, and, a little later, the Christian concept of dark night of the soul.

A *koan* is, in Buddhist thought, something like a riddle. A Zen teacher gives a koan to a student to break up the student's habitual patterns of thought and get him or her to push past barriers and inhibitions. A typical koan is the one about the sound of one hand clapping or the famous query, "What was your face before you were born?" I'm sure most people reading know this all from watching Bruce Lee movies or reruns of *Kung Fu*, but I want everybody to start on the same page before I shift the terms of the analysis a little.

I have been practicing Buddhist meditation since I was twenty-two years old, and, in the last fifteen years or so, I've been learning how to bring some practices from this tradition to bear on the daily life of teaching. My grounding in Christian spirituality, deepened at Shalem, has helped me commit to teaching as contemplative practice. When we are able to frame the problems of our teaching lives in the light of spiritual tra-dition, it seems to me that we have considerable ground for optimism. Our struggles make sense within such a landscape, with its Sloughs of Despond, its Valleys of Humiliation, and,

1

most significantly, its promise of radical transformation. On the other hand, when we see our lives within the models presented to us by popular culture, we head in the direction of breakdown. These cultural metaphors are mostly about buying and selling, packaging, consuming, and so on: the paradigms of business, in other words, which leave us at the end of the teaching day lugging our sample cases, like Willie Loman, through one more section of English 112. It's no wonder that *Death of a Salesman* has been revived on Broadway to new acclaim year after year.

Wendell Berry (1981), in his essay "Solving for Pattern," talks about the mischief that arises when business solutions, instead of agricultural solutions, are applied to the problems of farming. Similarly, teaching is, at root, a spiritual occupation, and the solutions to its problems have to be spiritual solutions. Most of us have always known this—teaching, like nursing and social work—attracts people who know this. What we do not know as young professionals, in the gentle light of what Zen calls "beginner's mind," is how dark the way will be. And, to be fair, spiritual concepts have, in the past twenty years, been marketed to western consumers in a facile way, advertised on the same glossy pages as BOTOX® and stretchy yoga outfits. "Things are tough," some Zen practitioners say, "so get up at 6 A.M. and meditate."

But, for many of us in education, things are worse than tough. My work has taken me around the country in recent years, visiting schools and talking with teachers. My colleagues tell me "things are tough *and* my partner beat me last night *and* my father's in home-hospice care *and* I have five preps." Being Teacher of the Year is not the goal for these individuals. Getting out of their pajamas before noon, when clinical depression lays them flat without adequate health insurance: that's the goal.

Let me quote here from a source I will return to over and over, Constance Fitzgerald's essay "Impasse and Dark Night":

By impasse, I mean that there is no way out of, no way around, no rational escape from, what imprisons one, no possibilities in the situation. In a true impasse, every normal manner of acting is brought to a standstill, and ironically, impasse is experienced not only in the problem itself but also in any solution rationally attempted. . . . The whole life situation suffers a depletion, has the word *limits* written upon it. . . . Any movement out, any next step, is canceled, and the most dangerous temptation is to give up, to quit, to surrender to cynicism and despair, in the face of the disappointment, disenchantment, hopelessness, and loss of meaning that encompass one. (1984, 94)

Forgive me for wallowing, if it seems that I am, in the data of how bad things can be. I do so because I don't think we can survive with any ease or grace if we do not admit to ourselves our despair and pain. Constance Fitzgerald is a Carmelite nun, an upbeat woman who tends to favor bright-colored contemporary clothing for her engagements outside the cloister. I've heard her say that her mission is to democratize the experience of Dark Night—which in western ascetic philosophy used to be thought of as the province of saints and mystics. But "We are [all] affected by darkness," she writes, "where we are most involved and committed and in what we love and care for most. Love makes us vulnerable, and it is love itself in its development that precipitates darkness . . ." (97).

In the workplace, for example. It's typical of a breakdown experience that all of our habitual ways of solving problems fail us—planning, organizing, reasoning, developing the five-paragraph grant proposal. Fitzgerald argues that "[t]horough-going impasse forces one . . . to end one's habitual ways of acting by a radical breaking out of the conceptual blocks that normally limit one's thinking" (1984, 96). Another contemplative monastic, Thomas Merton, put it this way, "Prayer and love are learned when prayer has become impossible and the heart has turned to stone."

We may not want to hear this, but if we do not, things get worse. The great, if pessimistic Kurt Vonnegut, announced on graduation day at Bennington College that "things are going to get infinitely worse than we can imagine" (1974, 162). I believe he did those Benington graduates a service. I think he told them the truth, and gave them a little bit of homeopathic medicine to carry them through. Things are bad, and they get worse when we deny our suffering and consequently limit our capacity for joy, insight, and breakthrough. We get stuck, then, in break-*down*. We need to stop, at such a time, retooling our five-paragraph equipment, reasoning even better, color-coding our closets, and, in general, rearranging the deck chairs on the Titanic, as Maryland's Senator Barbara Mikulski used to say. Instead, the task is to realize—from Constance Fitzgerald again—that "the unexpected, the alternative, the new vision is not given on command but is beyond conscious, rational control. It is the fruit of unconscious processes in which the situation of impasse itself becomes the focus of contemplative reflection" (1984, 96).

I'm struck by how similar this Christian theoretical framework is to the Buddhist analysis given me by my teacher, the Venerable Thich Nhat Hanh, when I was studying in his monastery in France, one winter of chilblains and rheumatism. Actually, Mahayana Buddhism doesn't bother much with formal koans. We do not have to worry about the sound of one hand clapping, because life presents us with personal riddles to practice: Why does your partner beat you? Why has the medical system abandoned your parents? Why do you have those five preps? Personal koans, according to my Buddhist teachers, are harder and more relevant than any meditation on "original face."

This brings me inevitably to the idea of practicing the koans of our daily life in teaching. Thich Nhat Hanh, in his dharma talks, would put it this way: *Mind is like a train on rails and the koan knocks out the rails so that we can find our true path.* This phrase gives me a conceptual frame inside of which I can choose to not shut down, to not anesthetize myself, to not despair, to not apologize, and to not be ashamed. Those, in my experience, are the traps. Those are the ways we get stuck in breakdown.

The Predictable Abyss of Life in Community

Several years ago my professional life was in a state of impasse:

> *November: Outside the window of my retreat cabin: nothing much; a red lacing of blackberry vine among brown twigs. I am trying to memorize the scene, stake out a territory of spaciousness in my mind to honor twenty-four hours when nothing at all has happened. Here is a ground of silence out of which new life may grow. I do not say that it* will *grow, for the essence of the Dark Night experience for most modern people is the way it undercuts our faith, fragile at best, in any redemptive possibility. We do not know if we are encircled by the* nada *of John of the Cross, or the* nada y pues nada *which writers like Ernest Hemingway articulated at the ground zero of Modernist nihilism.*
>
> *Six P.M. on a Minnesota winter evening yields infinite gradations of dark. The sky, deep gray, the quarter moon holds a light-streaked black disc, Scotch pines on the horizon. Even here, half way to boreal forest, "We are not educated for darkness. . . ."*
>
> *Most people turn to spirituality in hopes that it will make them feel better. Well, it will make them feel more: more joy, but also more bleak pain.*

At the time I wrote this journal entry, our department had ground to a halt as it has done periodically over the course of my long years of employment. Like individuals, communities go through the Dark Night experience, and like individuals they go through it over and over, either because they refuse to get the point or because there is always more to learn.

What I review here is an emergency recollected in tranquility. When I began to tell this story, I had not learned to see it as a spiritual passage, but simply as a disaster. Most days, I thought our departmental crisis of the moment was my fault; I blamed myself. Alternately, I thought it the fault of my colleagues: I blamed him and her and the collective. Yet, as I review the series of events that brought us to this crisis, it looks to me like the videotape of a delicately choreographed accident. No one involved could have acted differently and remained himself. Yet our actions brought us to grief, impasse, and breakdown. Not a single one of our coping strategies seemed to have any potential to work. We could imagine no future life together. It's interesting that such tragedies begin to borrow the dialect of divorce.

When one is locked in personal conflict, depressed or angry, sitting in a situation that has all the air sucked out of it, gasping, one does not feel oneself to be in a spiritual condition. But impasse is the essence of spiritual condition. Constance Fitzgerald has a resonant phrase for it, "homeward exile" (1984, 95).

English departments exist in a culture of judgment, which makes us particularly vulnerable to the assaults of darkness. When I remember how the nuns of my childhood warned us about "occasions of sin," these days I think about tenure reviews, rather than bars and the back seats of Chevies.

We are paid to find fault. Our idea of ourselves as dutiful, analytical colleagues is bound up with our relentless, faithful "marking"of student essays and collegial texts. And we struggle mightily—I hope!—to apply fairly rank-and-tenure policies susceptible of more nuanced interpretation than a metaphysical poem.

Analysis comes to a bleak landscape. In times of departmental impasse, our minds run obsessive programs: this is what he must be feeling, this is what she must think I'm feeling, here are the reasons why he deserved what he got, here are the mixed motives I fear in myself, here is how other people, if only they had acted wisely, might have avoided putting us in this situation—and what will happen in the future? Will we survive as a community? How much of the truth must be sacrificed to the ideal of common vision?

In the particular crisis I'm writing about—one could, of course, choose many others—the wisest discovery I made was the need for periodic physical retreat, sometimes to a cabin in the woods, sometimes just home to my pottery studio and the refuge of craft.

> *December*: *I tell myself over and over to sit still and keep breathing. Today, in my poetry class, we listened to different kinds of evocative sound, including ten minutes of Gregorian chant. So many notes for one syllable of a "Kyrie." That's the way to do it: put a lot of space around the problem.*

On top of all the difficulties of life in our department that year, we suffered an epidemic of lukewarm course evaluations. Teacher after teacher—those who were still speaking to me—was coming to my office in tears. Had we lost our collective skill-set? Was our entire range of techniques suddenly outmoded? Had the student demographic gone through one of its periodic shifts, arraying the young against us? We felt as though everything we used to be good at we were suddenly bad at.

In contrast to my students, who complained about being given too much freedom, one of my friend's students complained about her authoritarianism. What hurt this young professor so much was the cruelty of the written comments. I could only marvel at the account: she being one of the finest teachers in the department, one I would inevitably go to for mentoring about my own work. In my lighter moments, I would find myself humming a few bars of Gilbert and Sullivan: "That youth at us must have its fling is hard on us."

All of us seemed called into a deep and difficult collective practice, perhaps to bear the consequences of our judgments and inward cruelties. For certainly there are few *outward* cruelties in our department; incivility is rare. And we are most conscientious in our address to students. Gone are the days of scrawling *vapid generalization* on the margins of a student essay. Instead, we laboriously inscribe sentences like: "I would like to come away from this paragraph with a clearer sense of your central idea."

I wrote at the time, "It seems we are being punished more severely than our transgressions would warrant." I wrote that sentence, aware of its mysterious resonance, because it is a sentence that, in one form of articulation or another, I have heard from every person who confides in me at the deepest level; it is one of those scorched-earth statements of the human condition.

> *January: I've fled again to a hermitage in the woods. Tears of gratitude came to my eyes as I entered. It was so good to shake off the university, the Xerox machine, the pick-up truck that rode my bumper all the way from town.*
>
> *In my cabin this weekend I am reading Catherine de Hueck Doherty's,* Poustinia: Christian Spirituality of the East and Western Man *and Charlotte Joko Beck's book on Buddhist practice,* Nothing Special.
>
> *"Poustinia," I read, is the Russian word for "desert" and by extension, hermitage. Every Russian village, in the Czarist days, seemed to cherish a poustinia with its resident hermit. Such a person was not a recluse, necessarily, and certainly not a holy person. The "staretz" (or, feminine, "steritza") was just someone whose life story had made him available to listen, to help get the hay in before it rained, to practice hospitality.*
>
> *That seems a good job description for someone who wants to stay out of the fray and compulsive version-spinning of the average English department.*
>
> *Last night I suffered what's become a reoccurring dream, of trying to get somewhere but being too weak to walk. Fancy being tired while asleep! In this version I was lost in an old city with a circular courtyard in the center and many radiating streets going in all directions. I needed to get home; I was late already to give a seminar paper, but I was too weak to get there, confused, unable to explore all the possible avenues. I guess it was a dream about being lost in the labyrinth.*
>
> *Yet a labyrinth is a potent spiritual symbol, a puzzle, a koan. After some time in the labyrinth you win your freedom.*

Cherry Chocolate Cake

I think that the crises of professional life inevitably propel us toward freedom, though the nature of the freedom, for each of us, might differ because we struggle with different kinds of attachments. At a graduate-school level of struggle, our attachments may look like virtues, when in fact they are addictions. I, for one, used to soothe my inner anxieties by trying to put on a flawless classroom performance, write the most conscientious notes in the margins of my student papers, read collegial reports and white papers with helpful pen in hand. These might have been responsible contributions to the profession, but because I made them to medicate my insecurity and reinforce an image of myself as astute and organized, then they must be called addictions, or what Buddhism calls *attachments*. In saying this, I follow the analysis of my Shalem teacher, the psychiatrist Gerald May, who expounded the idea most skillfully in his classic *Addiction and Grace* (1998). It was Jerry, too, who introduced me to the writings of Constance Fitzgerald and reopened my reading of John of the Cross.

And not a moment too soon. There I was, freaking around in the labyrinth, feeling more incompetent than a T.A. lost in the echoing university cloisters—and I had committed to leading a workshop at Berea College on the spiritual foundations of teaching.

I remember those few days at Berea as a glimmer of dawn in the night passage I was making. Certainly not because I did a good job with my assignment—I arrived too cross-eyed with despair to make sense or even fake it. But breakdown is, perhaps, the primary condition for receiving grace. Those Berea teachers offered me three days of fabulous insight, and then gave me an honorarium.

We talked a little about some of the things I'd learned at Plum Village. Then I asked the Berea teachers, because I really needed to know: "How do you do this? How do you break the koan? How do you get out of your pajamas?" They gave me twenty minutes of good ideas and a recipe for cherry chocolate cake. One major point I carry forward from this encounter is: at some level we know how to dig ourselves out, and our colleagues can help us if we quit pretending everything's OK. Excuse me, it probably isn't.

John of the Cross wrote in the first book of The Dark Night: "If those in whom this occurs know how to remain quiet, without care and solicitude about any interior or exterior work, they will soon in that unconcern and idleness experience interior nourishment" (chap 2, no 2, qtd. in Fitzgerald 1984, 103). The seventeenth-century Quaker, Isaac Penington, wrote "Give over thine own willing; give over thine own running; give over thine own desiring to know, or to be any thing, and sink down to the seed . . ." (17). Similarly, the teachers at Berea agreed that the first thing we have to overcome is what one called "the struggle model of professional life," which informed our own education: the tendency to make ourselves so busy we can't think. One teacher said, "I have the idea I can make students listen if I just keep *pounding*. But in reality, that makes them shut down. They can't last more than twenty minutes." This woman was a professor of vocal music and she recalled that, "The great voice teachers do the same exercise over and over."

Another teacher made his daily mail run a site for mindful meditative walking. His colleague went home and did watercolor painting, badly I guess, because her point was: "It opens you to brokenness." Someone who lived with a severely disabled child said, "Just do the next thing. Be with."

When he spoke about solving the riddles of daily life, Thich Nhat Hanh said, "You have to let the koan settle into the deep storehouse of the unconscious. Respect it and pay gentle attention. It's a deep, long practice." Similarly, Meister Ekhardt wrote, "Seek God in error and forgetfulness and foolishness." I certainly don't know what collection of phenomena each of us might call God, but I do know that God's email address is foolishness.edu. The ceramic artist Paulus Berenson, one of my teachers, used to quote the Chinese proverb, "Art is what remains when the pot is broken."

I've confessed my addiction to perfection. Graduate school reinforces this habit of mind relentlessly. Most academic careers, if we are lucky enough to get jobs, are lived out in fear of the next collegial evaluation. The American academy is dominated by a pervasive fear that militates against creative thinking, or teaching, or even making a fashion statement. Yet all great spiritual traditions advise us, one way and another, to *screw up*.

There is a great deal of wisdom in the community on this topic, but you really have to look for it, because it is not fashionable wisdom. "We are not educated for darkness," Constance Fitzgerald says over and over. We are educated to keep doing what we were taught to do even when the meaning fails, the pot is shattered, the paradigm shifts: to keep pounding. We're like those World War II soldiers they used to find in the jungles of Borneo, twenty years after the war, still following the last order, keeping up the drill. If instead we can *stop*, cut back to the point where a few things can be accomplished with style and grace, to take the easy way (as Goethe advises), to take a nap—we will be open to the rewards of the Dark Night: the cherry chocolate cake, the new critical horizon, the radical relocation. Dorothee Soelle (1977) writes of "revolutionary patience"; she notes that its rewards are not only personal but societal. Quietly "being with" a problem, gracefully accepting limits: these patient and—may I say?—humble actions influence the course of civilizations more radically than all our pounding and perfecting. Constance Fitzgerald dreams of "a new and integrating spirituality capable of creating a new politics and generating new social structures" (1984, 114).

To bring this into our current national situation of despair and impasse, I ask, What if, on September 12, 2001, the president had declared twenty-four hours of silence? Maybe a whole week? *What if?*

Good teaching, not to mention the radical transformation of society, has to come out of our own peace. During the year of our deepest departmental impasse, I spent two days a month in the woods, which felt, to some of my friends, like a lot of vacationing. Just sitting. Yet, Thich Nhat Hanh would encourage us, "You sit for the world."

Off the Rails

Thich Nhat Hanh told us shivering novices, "Mind is like a train on rails and the koan knocks out the rails so we can find our true path." I'm trained to decode metaphors, so I want to know *What is the train? What are the rails? What is the true path?* How do we begin to answer these questions? In a certain sense, if we could answer any of those questions, we wouldn't be in trouble. If *mind* is the train, what are the rails?

In my years of attempted koanic thinking, I've come to understand that the rails are our habitual ways of thinking about a problem or issue. Since they are habitual, familiar gestures, it is hard to look at them analytically. To use that old but useful metaphor, the fish doesn't know about water because the fish is always swimming in it. Habitual ways of thinking are given to us by our parents, our education, our class and culture. We can't do without them, or we will—to name the only sin available in a psychologized culture—*behave inappropriately.* Yet often our habitual ways of reacting are dead stupid, or so circumscribed by some backwater culture as to be limiting in a larger vision of things. By *backwater culture*, I often mean, in the great scheme of intergalactic space, America.

I was taught, as a child, by my whimsical grandfather, that something terrible would happen if I bit into the hole of donut. I had to nibble around the perimeter of the thing, being careful not to break through the middle. Then I would appeal to my grandfather. "NOW you can eat the hole!" he would shriek with laughter, apparently unaware he was warping me for life.

I learned not only to avoid donut holes, but to eat most foods in a circle: sandwiches, Danish pastry. I still do it. Dead stupid. I think they can give you pills for this kind of behavior. But anyway, that's an example of what Buddhists call *bad habit energy* and psychologists call *faulty generalization.* It is at the root of many entrapments.

Cultural entrapments are even stickier than family scripts; there is such a web of ideas we weave into our personality, from good schools and bad schools, limited and expansive perspectives, small towns and big galaxies.

The particular details of crisis in my English department are unimportant, except insofar as they can help any one of us to see the rails—the attachments and entrapments—that force all communities to struggle through similar upheavals on a regular basis, as my experience suggests that they do. Because we need peace and civil order to do our difficult work, most of us repress annoyance, bite our tongues, and even bury deep philosophical disagreement on a daily basis. Things fester. Then, over some minor issue, chaos erupts and we find that the friends we thought we knew have become strangers to us. We have seldom, in the past, been real with each other; no mechanisms are in place to diffuse anger and admit uncertainty. Each of us struggles, suffers, and fights back in his or her accustomed, unproductive way.

John of the Cross, five hundred years ago, encouraged his monastic brothers to understand that "you have come to the monastery so that all may fashion and try you." He goes on to say that a community is full of *artists*; some "will fashion you with words, others by deeds, and others with thoughts against you." If you don't understand this, he concludes, "you will not know how to overcome your sensitiveness and feelings, nor will you get along well in the community . . . nor attain holy peace, nor free yourself from many stumbling blocks and evils" (qtd in Wolff-Salin, 1988, 41).

How well this describes the dynamics of the average academic department! Most of us do not come to teaching in order to be "fashioned and tried"; we are ignorant of how the members of small communities might abrade each other, and, in any case, graduate schools rarely teach us to view the crises of professional life as opportunities for spiritual progress. But if we can learn to appreciate the artistry of our colleagues' soul-making, we will reap the rewards of the Dark Night. When I look back on this bleak period in our departmental life, I think of it as a time when the universe decided to play badminton with me. Had I known it was playing badminton, even, things would have been better, but I thought it was playing hardball, or chess—like Death, in the old Bergman movie. That is, I thought I was an important person having a colossal series of problems, when in fact I was just a prairie Quaker having a colossal series of solutions.

In the Quaker world, we have a saying about the condition of impasse: "Way will open." In my case, way did not open. I became more and more isolated. At a certain point, of course, we learn to internalize shunning. The outside stimulus may have ceased but we are still walking around with downcast eyes and avoiding the reindeer games.

An insight came to me during this time of otherwise unproductive withdrawal, when I read the late journals of Thomas Merton. I've read Merton since I was a teenager, with some kind of strange attraction to the monastic vocation, feeling a call to the hermit's life, despite the indisputable fact that the Trappists don't take in girls. In recently published journals, Merton is characteristically honest about his cranky spiritual process. As soon as he achieved his hermitage, he began to chafe in it: it wasn't the right hermitage; he wanted a different view; he wanted Big Sur instead of Kentucky. I laughed at this restlessness, then recognized in it the mirror of my own. I wanted a hermitage, but not *this* one. Not *this* desert, please. I wanted a piney retreat in some scenic area. I didn't want to be abandoned in my third floor office while everybody else went to lunch. I didn't want to be excluded from the Friday night beer and pretzels or be kicked out of the gossip loop.

But then I realized that my third floor office was indeed a kind of hermitage, out of the crazy whirl of workplace politics. I exchanged unproductive withdrawal for a space of freedom. My exile was not punishment for some inadequate socialization, it was the answer to a barely articulated prayer. I thought I was in hell when, really, I was at Walden.

Mind is a train on rails. The rails here—the habitual way of thinking—had been built of cultural story: If you are a good person and try to tell the truth, you will have friends and be respected. I guess I learned this from my grandfather, who also made me eat in circles. Actually, if we try to tell the truth, it will get us in plenty of trouble at work, and not just because we are—as we would like to see ourselves—existential heroes and heroines. I believe, in my old-fashioned way, in the possibility of objective truth, but, on the darkling plain where English departments fight their battles, many *versions* can be in conflict, especially if we are not talking to each other very well or very often. Each one in turn may see himself as the heroic whistle-blower, punished for veracity; but, as often as not, we are punished for being egotistical, clumsy, unpracticed, rhetorically imprecise, or pathetically lacking in charm.

(Still, I think we should tell the truth.)

The psychologist Donald Winnicott helpfully questions whether professional life can survive anyone's best efforts to be whole. It's tempting to work this into a defense of the good person in the bad society, with oneself in the starring role, but instead I will just give it a big Minnesota *whatever.* Maybe I am the bad person in a good society, throwing swine before pearls, I don't know. It doesn't matter. What counts is that we come to understand the trap we are in and how our presuppositions about the nature of reality limit our perspective and cause us pain instead of working our liberation.

That's what I decided after years of practice in the *Night Desert,* to use the poet William Stafford's phrase. Nothing much changed in my workplace, except me. A few miles into the desert, I really wanted to get out of there. I thought it was going to kill me. Within the space of six months, I was hospitalized twice with sudden, serious illness. So the first thing I had to learn was how not to get sick. That's a good thing to know. How secure is anyone's insurance plan?

If the nature of this crisis was both banal and archetypal, so was its conclusion. Little by little, the situation stopped oppressing me, as I gradually become a person who couldn't be hurt by that particular set of circumstances—though I'm sure I will be challenged by the next koan the universe has ready for me. I'm grateful, in retrospect, for what I learned in solving that riddle: perhaps simply, as John of the Cross recommended, to overcome my sensitiveness. Pain is the tuition I paid.

March: I've been forty-eight hours in my poustinia. The time feels productive, though productive of what I find it hard to say. I've spent much of the weekend sewing and making little figures out of clay. I immerse myself in the nonverbal world, the domain of thread and clay. What's going on in our collective life defies analysis, and my only recourse is to open a trapdoor, at least, for subconscious knowledge to enter.

I feel like I am in a waiting, enduring space where nothing seems to be happening, a winter garden. That outside ground is frozen solid. But when the conditions for life return, something will start to circulate. Might as well hope it's blood.

If I say this year has destroyed me, what keeps that statement from being overdramatic is my belief that destruction is a good periodic practice; burn it all down to the dirt like a good prairie fire.

The patterns of narrative that drive our cultural story demand that now—for it's almost spring—some spiritual greening must occur. I should stage a resurrection if possible. But one does not slide so easily or gracefully out of the Dark Night. It's not hard to be born again; what's hard is staying born. Learning to walk in a new direction, talk a new talk.

April: I'm trying to stay with practice, just sitting. Buddhism at least gives you a posture and a method and doesn't ask you to fabricate emotions. Just being faithful to practice in the midst of crisis is excruciating enough. For me, the recurring temptation is to succumb to the cold comfort of my graduate thesis on Modernism: to say this is all without meaning.

And sitting is hard because it often flushes out images from the deep storehouse of consciousness that I don't want to look at. This morning a photograph rose before my eyes: myself as a child of three or four, standing in front of a house with my lost cousins. It renewed my longing to be in a family.

In communal crisis, each one endures solitarily the reprise of private losses. Knowing that, how can one not feel compassion for all of us in the department, caught in our old regrets and fears, enduring with such difficulty—and courage. For we are all at school, day after day, teaching as passionately as ever and nodding to each other with grave courtesy. Everyone comes to their "Terrible Sonnets" with only superficial differences in terrain. It doesn't seem wise to try to change things; rather, we are called to be with what is aching, which tooth. But it seems as if there will be no light ever again. That is the nature of this passage.

My sense of myself as a valuable participant in community life has been scorched down to the ground. I don't quite take this personally. To take it personally might be less metaphysically unsettling. The worst realization that comes to me is that of the radical loneliness of all human beings, the cruelty of any tribe. "It's not catastrophes, murders, deaths and diseases, that age and kill us"; as Virginia Woolf put it, "it's the way people look and laugh, and run up the steps of omnibuses" (Jacob's Room, 69).

"Prayer is an egg"—writes Rumi—"Hatch out the total helplessness inside" (2001, 104). If someone were reading me this journal, I'd say "At last! Our protagonist begins to learn!" She has come to the only condition genuine spirituality can address: the condition of destitution, nothing to gain. The only way out, at that point, is what Jesus called being born again, and as the Islamic poet imaged as being hatched.

I had overdone my job for years, as I only learned in the spring of that year when I reached a condition almost too weak to do it at all. I needed to retrain myself, difficult as it seems in a culture where overwork and mindless busyness are the norm. Why had I driven myself so hard? I think it was out of a desire to be loved and respected, so that people would lead me up the steps and into their house. Be my family. It worked, too; they liked me, they gave me tenure. Success made my attachment, my addiction to fellowship, stronger.

Why, against all the odds—I wondered in those days— *are classes going so well? I'm too preoccupied to think or plan properly. . . .*

However, I was learning to bring acute attentiveness to my time in the classroom. Pushed to the wall, I made everything up instinctively, figuring out at the end of each class where we needed to go the next day, keeping half an eye on next week. College teachers often forget that they have quite a lot of freedom; they don't use it. Sometimes I get bogged down in trying to teach to "the standards of the department" and fail to insist on *my* standards, which, though compatible, are not precisely the same. This inauthenticity had introduced a note of tension into the teaching day that is not present when one's work is congruent with one's deepest knowing. Deep knowing seems to arise when one's analytical barriers are torn down.

Yet even as insight came to me, I would get stuck again and again in "versioning"; analyzing, scolding, trying to settle on a story I could live with. The story one can live with is inevitably the ego's story, not the story that calls us to grow. I knew this, but I could not grow on a timetable that suited me. I had a hard time learning that the people with whom I was in contention were acting from internal logic different from mine. What they did made perfect sense inside their own frame of reference. What they considered bad I considered good, what I had time for they did not have time for—because they were working on something else, that I didn't have time for. Other people are not required to perform roles in one's internal play, no matter how wise, good, or reasonable the script may *seem*. Most of my unhappiness with my colleagues, never mind the President and Congress, comes out of my struggle with this fact.

My versions of this story usually permitted me to be angry. In the monastery, Thich Nhat Hanh was always trying to teach us that Americans overvalue feelings—especially what we call righteous indignation, which is simply anger in a socially acceptable disguise. Westerners seem to need anger as a motivator to action. But right action arises from clarity and focus, he would say, not indignation. Truly, some gifted people can intervene in a tumultuous situation with no more anger (again, Thich Nhat Hanh's image) than it takes to rearrange flowers in a vase. When I come to a place that I think of as "unhooked"—neither repressing a negative emotion nor riding it—such adjustments are easy. By contrast, when I am "hooked"—by fear, anger, or plain selfishness—I can't adjust a flower without its standing up on its stem and spitting chlorophyll at me.

Still, we should not be too hard on ourselves for our story-telling. We construct meaning out of our versions and myths. Each version is a little bit of wreckage we can float on to a place of safety. In fact, when we are deprived of our story, we are plunged into more chaos and fear; there is terrible suffering in the loss of foundational meaning. We are redeemed over and over from the situation of impasse by a return to first thoughts—but these fresh ideas are not likely to be happy ones when they come to us. We liked our old ideas very well. They worked for us. As we go through the process of disenchantment, surrender, and redemption over and over, we come to trust (!) the process of annihilation.

At the center of the Dark Night experience, we must inhabit the crystal sphere of paradox. When Thich Nhat Hanh encouraged us to *work justice without anger*, he spoke from a position of enlightenment, however tentative or tenuous any teacher's enlightenment may be. But no one can get to that place of serenity without *experiencing* his or her anger, sitting with it in a kind of mysterious love, knowing it like a beloved, naughty animal. One of my departmental colleagues swears by her therapist's advice, which is go home and beat on a pillow with her enemy's name attached. This is not an act likely to lead to compassion, or knowledge of your animal. Yet the worst thing—and people who follow a spiritual path often fall into this error—is to deny that anger exists. Every feeling must be settled down with, understood not with the mind but with the mature, accepting heart. Then, in the crystal of paradox, the feeling will not matter much.

Similarly, our salvation from the peculiar intellectual torments of the Dark Night will derive from first thoughts or new visions, but we survive in the short-term by clinging to our rather pathetic shreds of story and analysis. All around us the Big Ideas—about patriotism or marriage or religious commitments—may fall like trees in a straight-line wind, while we hang on for dear life to some tattered poem about, say, puppies and kittens. That's fine. Only, after awhile, let it go.

19

* * *

My crisis unwound through a Minnesota winter, and I did not make the train to resurrection on schedule, in spring. Unseasonably, in late summer, a friend gave me advice, patient and undramatic advice, that I was ready to hear. He was a man my age, who had traded a college presidency for the corporate world. Retiring as a CEO, he had this to say:

1. Take the initiative in building bridges.
2. Make friends in other departments.
3. Look for opportunities to mentor young colleagues and help unobtrusively. Be content to work behind the scenes.

Then he swiveled around on his office chair and told me the truth: "Look, Mary Rose, in the afternoon of a professional life we're called to radical renunciation. It's not a fecund, thriving time, but a solitary path of wisdom we're on."

Then he grinned. "The only consolation I have is to try out all the crazy ideas I can come up with! What can we lose?"

Reflecting on this difficult time, I have to ask myself why, for us modern people, the crises of the workplace have the power to shake us so. For many of us, I suspect, the professional world fills a place where church and family used to be. Unfortunately, it's not a *good* family, not a *nurturing* church— but it's all we can cling to.

Since this plague year, I've become, in my turn, pretty blunt in my advice to young people. To one struggling young man who talked to me I recently offered two choices: leave your job or find a spirituality broad enough to encompass its problems. Italo Calvino in *Invisible Cities* (1972, 165) speaks of the temptation, in straitened circumstances, to *become the inferno.* Instead, he says, we must find those things and people within the inferno who are not the inferno and befriend them. *That* is an example of a spirituality broad enough to encompass the problems of the modern workplace.

Human beings are wired for devotion. When I was a pre-school teacher, I was always surprised by how children spontaneously concoct things to worship. We teachers were always stumbling over their little altars in the playground. If we find no adequate object to worship, we seem to build an altar to any old false god. Work is the most common stand-in for a supreme being to offer sacrifice to; though patriotism is another reliable substitute. The old spiritual paths—like *bhakti yoga*—tried to channel our genius for devotion; early Christianity warned against spending our devotional energies on unworthy objects. It created the concept of *hyperdulia*: worship due only to God—which ought not to be expended elsewhere.

The experience of Dark Night, I now think, comes along to tell us we're worshipping an inadequate object. When it descends on us at work, it comes to loosen us from the bondage of a devotion we've offered to an unworthy object, a false god.

Nobody in This Lifeboat Looks Like Leonardo DiCaprio

Perhaps I had joined an English department unconsciously seeking something in this circle of gentle readers that was more than any workplace can or should give. If I am less idealistic about the academic world today, having withdrawn most of my projections, that is a gain, not a loss; it means I can live among my colleagues in amicable solitude and see us all more clearly for what we are. *What are we?* After such knowledge, as the poet inquired, what forgiveness?

I write at considerable psychic distance from the events narrated in this text. Memory, like the physical body, knows how to mend itself and heal. My friend and confidant, Mike Heller, of Roanoke College in Virginia, helped especially with a query about what he called *the constitutive metaphors that define life in an English department.* In trying to gather these metaphors, I am more aware than I have ever been of the conundrum of our lives together—and the compassion it might foster.

When, twenty years ago, I got tenure at what was then a small liberal arts college—later to discover the vocation of a dynamic and complicated university—the wife of one of my colleagues said to me, "We're each other's community now until we die." At the time I thought this a tender welcome. *Community*, for those of us coming of age in the sixties, was a warm and fuzzy word. Many of us had graduated from small colleges that used phrases like the "St. Trinian's family," which we undergraduates had been preironic about, except for those of us who were gay, or people of color, blue collar, suffering emotional illness, or in some other way subject to the Guess-Who's-Coming-to-the-St.-Trinian's-Family-Dinner-Table? syndrome. None of *us* were preironic.

Given what I knew from my small college about dorm life, why did I not realize my colleague's wife was warning me, that she was saying "Turn back, it's a trap"? Teaching English in a liberal arts college can be like hauling yourself into a lifeboat with twenty-odd other freezing people, none of whom looks like Leonardo DiCaprio. You are going to be there a long time, because nobody is hiring you away to a dream job at, say, Bennington, and you will spend your collegial time hitting other desperate swimmers over the head with oars lest they try to rock your boat, and occasionally throwing other rowers back into the icy water (these ritual actions are called hiring committees and tenure reviews). In your middle years, look around: you will have made hiring and promotion decisions on most of your colleagues. None of these decisions will be secret, because after every tense, confidential meeting your colleagues will likely have debriefed themselves at the nearest bar to campus. And you will be with these people until they figure out how to kill you.

Isn't it strange—this is the point I begin with—if we stand back and observe the data like anthropologists from the Planet Mongo—that we inhabit this hive of offices together (actually the stylemakers at our institution have renamed our new arrangement "pods")—all of us at different and mostly incompatible places in the life cycle, with many good reasons to dislike each other, and investment portfolios overweighted in TIAA-Traditional.

I can think of few analogous situations in the modern world, outside of a monastery or perhaps death row, where we are each other's community until we die. We survive this situation, where I come from, with the invocation of civility. *Civility* may mask years of brooding anger, fear, and hatred—or maybe lust and love. It has to be this way, I think, or there would be more lawsuits. This is America.

Mike Heller helped me over the years to conceptualize the peculiar ecosystem of the English department. He wrote an article inviting us all to think about the profession in terms of the famous words with which Dante begins the *Divine Comedy:* "Midway on our life's journey, I found myself / In dark woods, the right road lost. To tell about these woods is hard, so tangled and rough."

As I tried to do Mike's assignment, I began to think about this incarceration with my tenured and tenure-track colleagues—a graceful company, in my particular case, given the rigors of our journey together, but circumscribed and confined by the odd circumstances of our profession. I talked to Mike about what I was writing. We chatted about the dangers of this peculiar world: there are people you can come to write off, we can foreclose the possibilities for the growth and epiphany we hope to see in our students and admire as they are delineated in our texts, at least those texts written before 1950.

But I have to admit, as I wrote on and on about the lifeboat and the dark woods and the monastery and death row and the hive and the pods, I was not making myself happy and not only because I was mixing metaphors. Which is it, I demand of myself, a monastery or a prison? Some who have done time in monasteries might say, "Some choice." But I am thinking of St. Benedict's famous comment that the monastery is a school for love. It is not a school for civility, which is different, and good (and pagan—in Dante's scheme it would not even get us into the Purgatorio).

I am wary of adopting the monastic metaphor to my experience of departmental community, because it may seem (though only to nonmonastics) idealistic. We need to remember that, according to Benedict and his discourse community, a monastery is not a place where virtuous people go, but where people go who need for some karmic reason to be in school, people like us. Isn't it funny, most of us were the kids who were good at school, but we never get to pass. What happens in a monastery really (to borrow an image from Schopenhauer) is a lot of hedgehogs get thrown together in a gunny sack with their prickles at the ready.

When I feel most painfully the prickles of collegial life, I have to return to Constance Fitzgerald's analysis of the Dark Night phenomenon, to which I referred earlier. What I want to carry forward here is both the pain and the possibility of living professional life in terms of this radical analysis. What are we here for anyway? Not to repeat our tricks, like dogs jumping through a hoop of flame at the circus. The Dark Night experience forecloses every rational possibility that served one in the past. Frighteningly enough, this is a test good students can fail: we can give up, say we never meant it, repudiate our naiveté, and deconstruct our passion for meaning right out of existence. What moves me so deeply about professional life has been the example of some of my colleagues who have *not* given in to this temptation.

Permit me to repeat, in the manner of *lectio divina*, a few sentences of Constance Fitzgerald that I quoted earlier, in which she connects the Dark Night experience to our deepest hopes for the life we are given: "We are affected by darkness where we are most involved and committed, and in what we love and care for most. Love makes us vulnerable, and it is love itself and its development that precipitate darkness . . . " (1984, 97).

Most of us have lived lives of great commitment, loving and caring for a certain vision of academic life that seems to have been kidnapped in recent years by the culture wars, open admissions, and the hegemony of the business department. We have bumperstickers that say "I'd rather be reading Thomas Hardy" or "I Heart John Donne." We have loved and lost, in the best traditions of our discipline, and we have a legitimate right to bellyache. For these passions are more than the fashionable totems of graduate school, they are the structures of meaning and sources of identity most typically assailed by whatever relentless universal processes draw us toward higher levels of integration and wisdom. Call this beneficent assault, for the moment, *dark night of the soul.*

If we look back on the architecture of every paradigm shift we have been through in literary studies—beginning in classical times—we must surely acknowledge that each one has involved a breakdown experience, a dark night, for some constituency. People have *given their lives* in our discipline, as I keep politely reminding colleagues, over issues like whether freshmen should be allowed to write in the first-person singular. They have gotten cancer and died, they have gotten drunk and stepped in front of cars. Some of my more sanguine colleagues have solved this problem by simply announcing, "It's not worth it," and cutting their office hours for the golf green. But for others of us, this work is the architecture of our lives, a structure of meaning that supports our sense of self. For intelligent, disciplined people it's particularly difficult to engage a condition of impasse that challenges the habits of reason and organization that have served us well from graduate school on. It doesn't help—though I believe it's true—that the signals of breakdown are, simultaneously, the signals of imminent release and reorganization. (Somebody had to let go of requiring *Ethan Frome* in 101. Aren't you glad?)

When Constance Fitzgerald, Meister Eckhardt, John of the Cross, and Thich Nhat Hanh write about blockage and impasse, they describe in remarkably similar terms a time in life when things simply have to be held in abeyance. Agricultural metaphors abound. When I went through another experience of impasse recently—this time with our elder-care system—I became obsessed with the metaphor of "harrowing," which farmers used to do after the harvest and again before planting (these are Norwegians I live among): dragging a spiked chain over the fields to break up the clods so new growth can get through. All spiritual traditions recognize that you can't get to the sowing, much less to the harvesting, by wanting, whining, or taking drugs. We have to sit still and keep busy with unglamorous tasks and wait it out. Unconscious processes work themselves through on an internal timetable.

I wrote earlier about forgetfulness, foolishness, and broken pots—not popular topics of conversation in the faculty lunchroom. Most conversations I've heard about crisis in the discipline seem to feature metaphors of "manning the barricades" and "barbarians at the gates," of warlike defense, that is, rather than contemplation and surrender. The human suffering that attends the conditions of our profession is largely ignored. Yet, so many professorial stories—though they are rarely told outside of intimate space—circle around perceptions of betrayal or loss of innocence. How we guide and mentor each other through these crises of adult life may determine whether our companions emerge with deeper compassion and, in the best sense, sophistication, or sink into cynicism and loss of self-worth. True impasse defies our pomps and powers, as departments and as individuals, and leaves us weak and shamefast. It's not entirely respectable to talk about this sort of breakdown— "To tell about these woods is hard" as Dante wrote—but to remain silent is to risk annihilation in the dark.

In these remarks, I have been skipping through a lot of different metaphors for department life. What I think I am trying to do is answer this question for myself: what image of the department can I hold in my mind that will allow us the possibility of forgiving each other? In this venture, it matters what metaphors we use to describe ourselves to ourselves. A lifeboat. A pod. A hive. A monastery. An ecosystem. A minefield. What are your foundational metaphors about your department, and what are the consequences of them? How do they account for the best things that happen in your department and the worst? How do they make possible certain things that have to go on in a community of people who are going to be together until they die? I would like each of us to think about what metaphors we apply—perhaps almost unconsciously—to our English departments, and ask ourselves how these metaphors facilitate or obstruct its vital works: fostering the teaching mission; mentoring young professionals; creating a positive, recognizable, and communicable department culture; discerning gifts and encouraging the contributions of people of different talents.

What conception will allow people never to be written off, but always to have a chance to change? To let people be real with each other? To admit anger and uncertainty? To mediate inevitable conflict?

Proposing these standards, I must revise my text yet again. I renounce the first paragraph of this section! May I never grow so jaded as to suggest that the fundamental actions of spirit are more than any workplace can or should foster. Indeed, I have visited departments in which structures were firmly in place to support such a vision; writers like Parker Palmer have devoted a life's work to teaching people how to reconcile individual integrity and the concerns of the pod. "In fact," writes Parker Palmer, "when we live by the soul's imperatives, we gain the courage to serve institutions more faithfully, to help them resist their tendency to default on their own missions" (2004, 21).

So, in faithfulness, I refuse to let anyone off the hook, but will simply observe that forgiveness is central to all of these actions of the spirit. Sue Miller's novel, *While I Was Gone*, is about a woman who has to live in a small town alongside a man who killed her friend and got away with it. Maybe that happened in your department. This is what Sue Miller says:

Perhaps it's best to live with the possibility that around any corner, at any time, may come the person who reminds you of your
own capacity to surprise yourself, to put at risk everything that's
dear to you. Who reminds you of the distances we have to bridge
to begin to know anything about one another. Who reminds you
that what seems to be—even about yourself—may not be. That
like him, you need to be forgiven. (1999, 266)

Chapter 2

Softening Our
Relationship to Time

Chinese Tea

*T*he teaching life has strange phases, unlike the cycles of any other professional career: winter/summer, sabbatical time/crisis mode. It's almost as if the lessons of this vocation were set up to teach us the rhythms of going inward, going outward. . . .

It took me a while to learn to drink tea in the Chinese way. My early tea-training had been in little cafés and corner houses near the British Museum where I lurked during my graduate school sojourns in London. There, I learned to like my tea hot, strong, and milky. Many years later, I became a potter and learned to love the form of the yunomi, the Japanese or Chinese tea bowl, which is small and has no handles. But I had no interest in its function. The tea bowl felt good when I centered it on the potter's wheel. Fired and glazed and fulfilling its function, it would comfort cold hands. But the tea would be gone in one slurp and you couldn't carry it with you as you made phone calls and cleaned the house. As I learned to build the yunomi form, my house gathered a lot of containers for paper clips and miscellaneous coins.

Chinese tea was taught to me one afternoon in Portland, Oregon, when I sat in a tea house with a new friend, killing time—or, better, spending it. We ordered a strange-sounding brew.

"May I have milk, please?" I asked when the dark tea arrived in its tiny bowl.

The Chinese waiter responded, "We do not use milk and sugar." Instead, I received a small bowl of jasmine-and-green tea, as I would say, "black," but, as the Chinese might say, "infinitely dappled and giving birth to a multiplicity of form." My server suggested we "smell the jasmine," and went away. I smelled the jasmine and watched the tea buds unroll and stretch into sinew, shred, flag, sea weed, creature, flower. I sipped what I thought would be tasteless, but which was, in fact, delicate. The ceremony engaged each sense in turn; the hand cupping the bowl was as pleased as the eye and the nose.

Chinese tea in a Chinese tea house is the tea of mindfulness. I could not help but be acutely present to the graceful proportions of the room, to my companion's soft responses. We had sat down to kill time—violent phrase—but instead we drank bowl after bowl of time, pure grace. Just as the tea got a bit strong, the server reappeared with hot water and the tea's flowers bloomed again, releasing jasmine and flavor enough to fuel twenty minutes more of conversation.

Our tea house ritual in the Western city continued an hour or more, and never lost its piquancy. I came home to Minnesota and my potter's wheel ready to make a new vessel for my friends, not a receptacle for spare change and paper clips but a cup of respite and joy. *Here is a quiet moment, fragrance, warmth, and we are together.* I think about my friend, Jim Thomas, who gave away a thousand raku bowls from his potter's wheel, rather as one would make a thousand cranes.

This kind of tea—the right bowl, the right leaf, the friend—creates a Sabbath of spirit. We talk about union breaks and coffee breaks, but we seldom really break for our guilty pleasures. We drink coffee whilst checking our email or drag a cup around the house from chore to chore. The great advantage of smoking—to focus on the guiltiest of pleasures—is that you are more likely to have to *stop* and do it. In Minnesota, you have to stop, go outside, and secrete yourself in a vacant lot. It has a lot in common with Irish monasticism, especially in winter: the secluded site, the inclement weather, the reluctant trek into the wilderness of monastic comrades. You have to stop, as I said, and you have to breathe. In fact, the only way I managed to quit smoking was to realize that what I was really craving was a deep breath. That realization, some thirty years ago, may have been the beginning of my meditation practice. The French have a saying, "To smoke is to pray." That captures the idea. So smoke if you must, or better yet, go outside and pretend to.

A young clerk gave me a fine gift one day when I was fumbling around in my purse looking for change at an inappropriate moment. "I have all the time in the world," he told me. In my family of origin, by contrast, the mantra was "Hurry up! Hurry up!" My father was always trying to get us to church on time. We even had a pet parakeet that learned to cry out "Hurry up! Hurry up!" The parakeet's name was Beauty, which he could also shriek. The latter phrase was more useful. *Beauty! Beauty!* The folksinger Michael Cooney used to say that he wished they'd test the air raid sirens at sunset, to call everyone to come out and look. *Beauty!*

Thich Nhat Hanh often suggests the metaphor—or the task—of doing dishes to do dishes: some simple physical work that focuses the mind and pulls us into the present. I thought I had a fix on this "doing dishes to do dishes" thing, until the master potter Warren MacKenzie opened up a whole new dimension for me. Public TV made a documentary of *him* washing dishes in his kitchen, holding each vessel up to the light, "Oh, this is an Edo tea bowl. This mug is by Bernard Leach . . . M. C. Richards gave this to me for my birthday."

Beauty! Beauty! It made me long to get my hands in the soapsuds.

How to Be Mindful When Your Mind Is Too Full

I know how to practice *mindfulness*—that exquisitely simple and complicated way of contemplative presence. That is, I've been well-trained in it almost from childhood, studying at such disparate spiritual sites as my grandfather's carpentry shop, a Catholic novitiate, and a Buddhist monastery. But I fail, on a daily basis, to practice well. Daily, I hope to succeed in practicing it better. Daily, I mess it all up.

I was thinking about this rhythm of success and failure, most recently, in the dentist's chair. For so many of us, that biyearly appointment with the hygienist is the one place in life where we have to sit still. On this particular occasion, I had only remembered my appointment around 10 A.M. in the morning. Because I had left no space in my day to sit in that dental chair, I cut my morning yoga. Rushing to a faculty meeting, I skipped lunch and ate some deep-fried thing later in the school cafeteria. I missed swimming my laps with a friend; I failed to "hang out" with a student when he asked. "I'm on deadline," became my excuse all day. The hygienist, when she got hold of me, informed me, as if I didn't already know, that I wasn't flossing every day, in that crabby way they have, as if she had taken on the whole social burden of guilting people that used to be shared by clerics and English teachers.

Isn't it boring to talk about how busy each of us is? How are you finding the time it takes to read these sentences? I hope you aren't neglecting something really important, like flossing.

In amicable contrast to what I wrote earlier about softening time, I am wondering how to be mindful when the mind is already too full. Most of us have heard the news that spiritual practice might be good for us, might lower blood pressure, might help us to sleep better. But we think we don't have time. Recently there's been a vogue for carrying water around in a bottle all day to maintain some optimal level of hydration. These are people who don't have an afternoon to give to Chinese tea! I can't tell you how many women confide to me that they ignore this fashion for drinking water because they don't have time to pee.

My point here will be that—although one might not have time for Chinese tea or for yoga, or even for flossing—any one of us has time for mindfulness practice, every day. Not perfect practice, not the strong practice my teachers honor, but at least a certain *je ne sais quoi* discipline. In mindfulness practice, everything that gets in the way is the solution, not the problem; therefore, it is the wonderful reverse of other things in life we struggle with.

When I spent time in Thich Nhat Hanh's monastery in France, one thing in particular surprised me: no one ever apologized for anything. Except me, of course. In Minnesota, if you bump somebody accidentally, you apologize and *they* apologize. You have a whole little responsorial Lutheran liturgy over it. At Plum Village, I said I was sorry to one of the Vietnamese sisters for having completely disrupted her lunch preparations with some stupid obstructive action. She said, "We don't apologize. It's to practice."

I would like to begin on this phrase, "It's to practice." In mindfulness discipline, everything that obstructs and impedes and annoys is *to practice*. It's a lesson from the universe, a correspondence course, pass/fail.

So there I was at the dentist, watching my breathing. Scrape-scrape-scrape. Watching my breath. *Discomfort is merely sensation*, I said to myself. *Be aware of it. Breathe it in. Don't go to Hawaii in your mind.*

Do you know what? I was not succeeding at this practice in the dental chair. I certainly had no inclination to be truly present to that relentless scraping. But my failure got me thinking, at least, about how we might learn to succeed. To quote Michael Cooney again, "Life is a series of timed tests." I was failing, oh, graduate school. For me, for everyone I think, meditating in the midst of physical pain is the most difficult advanced practice.

We need a series of small exercises, warm-ups, to get ready. In Minnesota, I suggest to my meditation students that they practice the weather. Don't scrunch up against the cold. Walk happily. Don't slip on the ice. That is our drill from November to March. It's a nice little introductory exercise. In California, I guess, people could practice the power outages.

What I wish to present in this chapter are a few things I've learned about simple, daily practice. I assume that everyone reading this book has some experience with meditation and knows a little about mindfulness meditation, just sitting still and watching the breath. If not, well, just sit still and watch your breath. That's the vipassana technique, just watch the breath go in and out. In Zen sitting, students learn to count breaths. In the Hindu tradition, they say a mantra. I'm assuming everybody knows this much, so I merely offer a quick review. But in case there's somebody reading who's never heard any of this before, you aren't behind. We spend our whole lives just learning to be with the breath. Western meditators have come to call this *mindfulness practice*, and I shall be extending this concept a little and talking about ways in which we can carry mindfulness into the world, even into the traffic, if you will. Most of us know that it's not too hard to be mindful, or centered, or grounded—choose your metaphor—at home on the zafu or in a rocking chair with the cat in your lap. But the real test of life is at 5 P.M., when you're picking up the kids from daycare, your daughter tells you she has an earache, and you remember that you're out of bread, milk, and toilet paper. Or it's one of those little timed tests.

In the daily circumstances of a busy life, what seems to me most essential and lifesaving is walking meditation. In many Buddhist traditions—and in Christianity as well, if you explore the deep roots of practices like the Way of the Pilgrim or the Stations of the Cross—there is some kind of walking practice. This may be slow walking in a conscious way, or walking at a normal—but "mindful" pace. Mind empty. Mind in the feet, no higher than the kneecaps. You can follow a mantra as you do this, if you have trouble just being present in your feet: Thich Nhat Hanh suggests the words: *arrived home, arrived home, arrived home*. In the orthodox Christian tradition, the repetition is *Jesus Christ, Son of God, Savior*. Quakers resonate to George Fox's famous phrase, "Walk peacefully over the earth, answering to that of God in everybody." You can turn to a visual image such as planting a lotus with every footstep. I was surprised to hear one my Minnesota students say how meaningful this image was to her, as I can't imagine she's ever seen a lotus. "I feel like my feet are walking deeper than the sidewalk," she told me, those sidewalks covered in three inches of ice.

In Zen communities, sitting meditation is central. I didn't encounter walking mediation until I studied at Plum Village. At Thich Nhat Hanh's community, we would sit for twenty minutes, walk for five, sit for twenty, walk again. I thought that walking was just a way of unkinking your body from the sitting. I almost missed the point that walking meditation is *the* central practice of Plum Village; it's more important, I would venture to say, than sitting meditation. The variant of Mahayana Buddhism that Thich Nhat Hanh developed during the Vietnam War emphasizes being active in the world. This kind of Buddhism is oriented to social justice work, connected to it, in love with it. Walking practice is the way you go into the world, on your feet, and the way you stay in the world, on your feet, attentive, loving, warming to the pavement. It has a beautiful ripple effect. One person practicing conscious walking on a college campus, or in a mall—or, as one of my students tried to do, in Treasure Island Casino—can shed waves and waves of peace. You begin, when you're doing this, to notice how much pain and distress surrounds you. You see the agonizing forward momentum on so many faces. Thus, walking practice inevitably leads you to deeper compassion.

I would like to pause in my mind here and dedicate what I'm saying to the memory of my father, who hated anything he called "oriental," or anything Buddhist, which he dismissed as "navel gazing." He had contempt for any religious exercise, including those of his own Catholic tradition, that took a person out of the world. But walking meditation, by contrast, is a socially involved practice, one that allows you to carry your hermitage with you. Everyone you meet can benefit from it.

Walking meditation revealed its central importance to me in the days after the 2001 attacks. On September 11, my first impulse was to go to my university and simply *walk*. I'm asking, I know, an act of faith here from people to whom this practice is unfamiliar. Can something as simple as walking meditation truly be a response to the psychic insult of a terror attack? Yes, I would guardedly say, especially if your walking is a deep and conditioned way of being in the world. You don't have to be a meditator to practice this calming demeanor; it is, in some way lost to many of us, natural. I've seen beat cops, intensive care nurses, and veterinarians offer a similar gift to the workplace. In my town, I watch the Somali immigrant women going their dignified daily round, and sometimes I walk behind them, putting my feet in their footsteps the same as I used to try, literally, to follow Thich Nhat Hanh.

Related to walking meditation is a practice some Buddhist and Yogic traditions call *body scanning*. This simple exercise involves moving the attention through one's body, looking for patterns of holding and resistance, then methodically letting them go. We do not often remember that teaching is a kind of public performance, with three or four shows a day to put on, and we teachers are insufficiently trained in the techniques actors use to stay loose in the spotlight. In the middle years of professional life we become aware of the deformities created by hunching our shoulders or crouching behind the lectern. Body scanning helps us not to get literally bent out of shape.

Body scanning is not a self-involved practice, either. For the last few years, I have been working as a volunteer in wildlife rehabilitation, taking care of squirrels and foxes and coyotes that have been brought into a veterinary hospital after encounters with cars and hunters. I'm used to being attentive to animal behavior. That way you don't get bitten as often. We human animals also cringe in fear and tense in anger; our bodies act out discomfort and shyness. Other animals can sense the emotions we're socialized to hide. We need to practice conscious release and surrender if only so we will not *scare* each other so much. And remember to be there, at home in your body. People who teach self-defense courses say that attackers look for the distracted victim. The last thing you need at 5 P.M., when you're rushing your daughter to the urgent care clinic, is to get mugged.

In framing these practices of awareness, I remember that the Buddhist way asks us to see every person as our dearest spiritual teacher. So, if you're getting annoyed at that commuter poking along on the freeway, you can soften to him or her, see the fellow driver as your teacher. My spiritual director tells me that gnostic Christians used to translate the famous Greek text, *Love your neighbor as yourself* this way: *Love your neighbor, he is like you.* Or, your neighbor may have a hot-dish on his lap. This insight came to me from a Quaker friend who arrived breathless at a pot luck (which is our sacrament, for those in the know). He told me, "I know I was making other drivers crazy. I had this tuna hotdish on my knees—the kind with the potato chips on top, sloshing with cream-of-mushroom soup. I had to drive slowly, accelerate with care. I had on my best trousers."

So now when somebody is driving me crazy in traffic, accelerating slowly and piddling along at the speed limit, I try to remember he may have a hotdish on his lap. In Britain, they have signs for the rear window of a new car that says "running in," so other drivers will cut them some slack. I want a bumpersticker that says, "I have a hotdish on my lap."

In general, I like to do things slowly, and I like quiet. But sometimes it's instructive to do exactly the opposite, especially when you have company coming for dinner. Run around like crazy. We all know how to do this. Then the hard part: stop. Freeze tag. Feel the organism. Or immerse yourself in sound—this, too, is readily available—then seek silence. This is how Rinzai Zen monasteries practice, I believe. When I'm teaching literature, we often practice *lectio divina*, which involves reading very small snatches of text, stopping, and pondering, as though each poem were a sacred text. But sometimes, just to be contrary, we practice Rinzai Zen instead. I give my students a big chunk of Foucault or something and ask them to tear through it, just putting a check in the margin where they think something important might be happening. The *lectio* method helps us to get deeper into the sacred space of texts, but let's not be precious about it. The opposite method—if only for contrast—helps us to value the silence and the open space.

It is perhaps not widely enough recognized that most healthy contemplative traditions were designed to be practiced in the midst of noise, because noise is *what is*. For me, contemplation has been not a retreat but a path of tender emergence into the world. Spiritual practice has helped me, a shy and introverted person, to enjoy parties, to brook hostility, to find voice, and to get out of the house as a passionate environmentalist and amateur naturalist. The contemplative does not resist the world, but learns to enter it.

There was an attender in my Quaker meeting who complained constantly about the noise children made in meeting and how it interfered with her prayer. With respect, I think she was off track here. Jesus, we know, surrounded himself with children, but sometimes he had to go into the desert to get rid of the adults. For, certainly, we can lose the pulse. Finding a quiet center in the midst of people is a graduate exercise, like going to the dentist. I think the most difficult kind of practice—next to prison—is in the midst of a party, especially one of those faculty or work affairs that is like a medieval morality play of the Seven Capitol Sins. There you are belly up to the chip dip with Lust and Gluttony, attempting polite conversation. You can feel assailed, kidnapped, especially if you don't have tenure. One of my quiet friends remarks about such conditions, "I feel that I lose myself."

Yes, I think that at such times the self can leak out like air from a tire. Watching our breathing, we become aware of the rise and fall of being, of mind. It's like watching an underground sea rise and fall. When, by contrast, we lose focus, it's as though the sea rushes out of us. Maybe this is what psychologists mean by *boundary issues*. The walls of our spirit are broken down, our inner sea rushes out, and we are overwhelmed by the inrush of all the contaminants of a toxic culture. Sensitive people are vulnerable to this kind of assault. Perhaps it's what John Donne had in mind when he wrote his poem, "Batter my heart, three-personned God." He compares himself to a city that has been surrendered to the enemy; he begs God to defend his boundaries. Similarly, Thich Nhat Hanh says, "Don't let yourself be colonized."

The greatest mistakes I have made in teaching and in life have involved overreaching my limitations, opening too much. I don't think I'm alone in this (although, for others, the task might be opening at all). My young friends and students who go out into the helping professions are ready to—in the Quaker phrase—"try what love can do." Often I know their families, and participate in the circles of affections and support that sustain these young people and give them the daily courage to do the work of the Peace Corps or Teach for America or other national service. But as Harvey Cox used to remark, it's hard to be I/thou with a whole city.

One problem is that most of the opportunities to serve that our culture holds out are severely compromised in their integrity. Every spring I write letters of recommendation for my best students as they enter such vocations, fearing that they will fetch up a year or two later, bruised, perhaps cynical, and thoroughly exhausted. Such programs in education, health, and social services showcase the idealism of young America, but, all too soon, the young Americans discover that they are being offered insufficient practical support to create a viable community and get the job done. Into this inferno go my young students, bearing *love*.

It's possible to survive such conditions if you learn not to pour yourself out, to use Augustine's phrase, like water upon sand. In my own early teaching I made the mistake of thinking that my interest in and concern for troubled students could outweigh the effects of soul destruction that had begun well before that young person appeared in school. One can work tirelessly for many years in such contexts, trying to save a few kids, but after a while one simply gets tired.

My friend Peter Crysdale, who pastors a small, rural congregation in Massachusetts, always reminds me about what he calls The Cloak of Protection. This is an old religious image, common to many traditions. I have to remember to wrap myself in this metaphor when I venture into dangerous territory—and any territory can turn dangerous if one is inattentive.

What are we doing here in this perilous world? Peter and I call it *guerilla contemplation*. As a young person, I was always trying to find my monastery, some secure and quiet place where I could be at peace. Like Gerard Manley Hopkins— himself an inner-city minister—I longed to be "where springs not fail," "where no storms come" (5). But I know now that such a sanctuary must be built within this body we are given, within the world as it is. We must not mistake introversion for a call to permanent retreat. The world is not going to quiet down because one is shy and needs some time in the bathroom with the magazines. Once I figured this out I became quite the little contemplative party animal. Parties are, in fact, one of the best places (as the nuns of Plum Village might say) *to practice*.

So let's return to that departmental soiree, back to the chip dip. What now?

Watch your breath. Watch the rise and fall of the self. Watch it skid to the edge of its boundaries, gently calling it back. Listen to Anger tell what he thinks of the department chair. This is hard practice. In my book *The Barn at the End of the World*, I told a story about how a young Russian student accosted one of the most revered members of the Plum Village community, Sister Anabel, and demanded an account of all her years of contemplation. "Sister Anabel? Have you succeeded in practicing anger?"

There was a moment of silence, then Sister Anabel leaned forward. "No," she said, "That is why I remain."

Parties, the dentist, dissertation defenses, tenure reviews, muggings: these require advanced mindfulness practice. But the foundation never changes, watching the breath, walking mindfully. Being with the world. Breathing.

Still.

No matter how adept we come to be at running practice, driving practice, or grading-essay-practice, we must create a sacred space in the day for time on the zafu of our choice. Every religious tradition tells us, mysteriously, *pray always*. "Let the fire of your prayer burn always on the altar of your soul" (1979, 321), writes the desert father, John of Karpathos. I long to dissolve the historical barrier between the active and contemplative vocations, but I cannot surrender quiet, slow time: Chinese tea, retreats, sabbaticals, and sabbaths. In a sense, these are not mine to give away. When I begin to slight my daily half hour of sitting meditation, the fire in my soul starts to gutter and go out. Someone at Plum Village told me that an emissary from a group of physicians and lawyers who belonged to the Order of Interbeing came to ask Thich Nhat Hanh to reduce the requirement for a monthly retreat day. All these busy people complained that they just couldn't find time. Thich Nhat Hanh thought about the problem for a few months and could not—which is rare for him—find an accommodation. "Without this retreat," he told them, "it is simply not possible to do the work."

Paradox again. The discipline of daily and monthly intensive practice is essential to my life. I find that out, again and again, as I find out everything, by screwing up, letting myself be kidnapped by some glamorous crisis or the need to find quality time with a new Border collie. But I also know that we don't have to withdraw from the world to tend an esoteric fire. Mindfulness, really, is our birthright. It is who we are. Annie Dillard writes, "Experiencing the present purely is being emptied and hollow; you catch grace as a man fills his cup under a waterfall" (1974, 81). Although our cups can only take a little in, the waterfall itself is inexhaustible.

Chapter 3

Prophetic Witness and Mourning in School

The Mystic, the Prophet, and the Rhetorician

In the midst of writing about mindfulness practice at work, I felt a flare of anger, that dangerous emotion that I, like Sister Anabel, experience and cherish for its illuminating lessons. I remembered how often spiritual practice has been offered to abused and suffering people to keep them down on whatever plantation they happened to be languishing. Suffering people of the moment—though let's keep it in perspective—might includes T.A.s, adjunct profs, most rhetoric teachers, and, in fact, any teacher with more than fifteen students in the room. (This happens to be the number at which, I'm told, enrollments have been capped in Cuba since the revolution.) I hope that what I've written will help teachers to breathe and nourish their sprits so that they can stay reasonably gold for the long haul, succumbing neither to despair nor quietism.

Contemplative practice offers a rational site for social analysis, and the classroom remains for me an environment where it's possible to carry out both transformative experiment and prophetic witness. The more graceful modes of argument and persuasion, especially those grounded in Rogerian principles, are so essential to the stability and civility of our international conversation that I wonder why English teachers spend so much time playacting the dramas of collegial life instead of getting out of the faculty meeting and into the agora. But that is a subject for another day. For now I want to concentrate on the less well-advertised rhetorical structures of mysticism and prophecy.

There are numerous languages in tension, in our homes, our universities, our classrooms, and our texts; there are so many ways to understand and misunderstand each other. Some of them are as new as the vocabularies of postmodern criticism, feminism, or queer theory, others as ancient as an inscription on fifth-century papyrus, something perhaps by Sappho or Buddha, which—despite its ancient context—hooks the modern reader. ". . . there is no place that does not see you. You must change your life." Rilke (1989) wrote of such an encounter with the fragments and potsherds of culture.

I would like to think about three modes of rhetoric that are especially and inevitably in tension: the *legal*, the *mystical*, and the *prophetic*. We tend to confuse the claims of each not only in religious culture, which is not my province here—although it was contemporary Biblical hermeneutics that energized me to start thinking about these distinctions—but also in professional culture, which is my province.

Legal discourse is the most familiar of these rhetorical worlds; it is central to our professional self-understanding. Our collegial dialogues are grounded in rules, catalog descriptions, departmental handbooks, graduation requirements, and so on. The cadres of lawyers most colleges now employ assure us that these documents have a quasi-legal status, which I guess means "legal" when you want it to be and "quasi" when you don't.

Mystical language is more challenging to us, because it privileges ways of knowing that have not usually been admitted to professional conversation—although this and similar covert discourses—political, for example, or erotic—create a pressure that moves systems in ways we pretend to be ignorant of. The philosopher Simone Weil (1977, 23) called mysticism "the language of the nuptial chamber," conflating it in an interesting way with erotic discourse. Therefore, she tells us, we should not expect to understand the language of the bridegroom in the same way as we understand the patter of those selling trinkets in the marketplace.

Thinking about these worlds of language leads me to wonder about the kinds of spaces we are able to create in the classroom for certain kinds of words to be heard. One of my mentors, the Native American poet Barney Bush, tells me that when he reads poetry, he has to go into his house in the deep woods and create a silence that matches the silence from which the writer wrote. Is there a way we can do that at school? Should we install reading rugs, perhaps, like they have in progressive kindergartens?

In making these initial distinctions, I wish not to privilege any particular level or key of discourse. Lawyers are easy targets in one kind of departmental enclave, as mystics might be in another. Yet I think about how, in *A Man for All Seasons*, the playwright Robert Bolt taught us to negotiate with his protagonist Sir Thomas More "the thickets of the law," Thomas More being, he tells us, "a forester" (1962, 37). The law assists "our natural business," which More goes on, "lies in escaping" (73). Not that there is anything to escape from around our colleges and universities. Not that there is any violence to avoid. Not that there is anything to fear.

But legal language is fairly familiar to us and I will leave it aside to concentrate on the place of mystical and prophetic language in professional discourse. I hope, among other things, to reclaim higher ground for the word *mystic*, which has been tossed around a lot on shows like *Buffy the Vampire Slayer*. (If you do cultural studies, you have to watch a lot of TV.)

Mystical discourse is not necessarily religious or metaphysical conversation. That we limit it this way is one of the reasons we don't read it well when we meet it in a secular context.

One year, at my university, we chose the poet Mark Doty's memoir *Heaven's Coast*, as our common text, which meant that all of our freshman students read it in English class. We selected the book—which recounts the death of Doty's partner, Wally, from AIDS—as part of a curricular initiative that requires us to represent different valences of diversity. *Heaven's Coast* presented a few problems for our students, though not as many as we had anticipated. Many of these problems, I'd suggest, had less to do with homophobia than with understanding mystical discourse. Doty keeps reminding us that what he's trying to say is essentially *unsayable*. Most poets, one way and another, make this point, along with most bridegrooms. All of us, even if we are not poets, know, from our own experience, this terrain of the unsayable. And if we can place ourselves in recollection, for a moment, on this ground, then we may rest in the knowledge that each of us knows a lot about mystical communication.

Doty crosses this space between the unsayable and the text by a process he calls "dreaming into images." My colleagues and I found it challenging to teach students what was for many an unfamiliar way of knowing. That we set out to do so justified, for me, much of that quasi-legal language in the university catalogue. Our distribution requirements acquaint students with mathematical and scientific and sociological ways of knowing; here in English young people were being initiated into an essentially *mystical* way of knowing.

Reading Doty, students had to follow their intuitions and suspend, from time to time, a logical analysis. Student after student shyly reported that they intuitively found *Heaven's Coast* to be a profoundly spiritual book. But we had to suffer together through that tension of languages-in-conflict that I referred to earlier. Mine is a conservative Catholic university. Every summer I, as a freshman adviser, get phone calls from anxious parents wanting their son or daughter assigned to sections of freshman English that won't challenge their faith. A misguided aspiration, the most faithful of us might agree, but one that made that year's choice of common text problematic. We could quickly sense in our classrooms the familiar patterns of breakdown that precede breakthrough, breakdowns particularly rooted in language: in how things are named. What is a student to do if he, on the one hand, intuits a spiritual

presence in the text, while, on the other, catechetical discourse—a variant of the legal—warns that the book is "an
occasion of sin"? We got a lot of nasty phone calls.

We had the great honor of having Mark Doty visit campus
and attend classes. He said he felt as though he had a sign over
his head that read, "visiting homosexual." Yet students were
pulling at his sleeve and begging him to address himself to the
religious questions they perceived in his work. Doty, at such
moments, had the look of a man experiencing his own form of
cognitive dissonance; yet he shared with us three habits of
mind that he considered necessary to a spiritual outlook. They
were the ability (1) to pay acute attention; (2) to inhabit paradox; and (3) to resist certainty—to "live the questions," as
Rilke put it.

These are three habits of mind that we need to comprehend
mystical, discourse, or poetry, or to dream into the images of
literary nonfiction, or read certain kinds of student journals.
They represent intellectual attitudes often neglected and
undervalued. When we defend what we do in the classroom—
as we so often have to do with our frequent restructurings of
the liberal arts curriculum—these qualities do not often come
to mind. I think they should.

Years ago, before the theology faculty thought better of it, I
used to teach an interdisciplinary course for which freshmen
got credit in both English and religious studies. It was while
moving back and forth between theological texts and literary
texts that I began thinking about the different kind of truth
claims implicit in each. Legal, mystical, and prophetic discourse lie cheek by jowl in Hebrew and Christian scripture,
and the astute reader must learn that different discourses make
different demands. Religious texts are those that most obviously try to deal with the unsayable—although the first sym-
bolic equivalent of a mystical intuition may be stuttering or
stammering or silence or music rather than words.

As soon as these stutters and stammers get into the hands of
the leaders and intellectuals who have to parcel them out for

community consumption, we get categories, analysis, taxonomy, Deuteronomy, and every other sort of legal discourse. If the requisite attitudes necessary to the birth of mystery are attention, toleration of paradox, and resistance to closure, the requisite attitude necessary to the birth of law is, perhaps, obedience. Obedience makes for social order. It frees us from the burden of attention and the anxiety of paradox. It makes spiritual insight bearable and comprehensible to a majority of consumers.

Mystical discourse, then, can quickly jell into legal and catechetical language. Such a domestication is culture's primary defense against the mystic's implicit demand for change. I think that farther down the lines of communication, we discover an increasing hardening of language in the discourses of fundamentalism. We find a conflation of sign and signifier, to use the language of the poststructuralist nuptial chamber. It's not that I find *faith* hard to understand; I find *trust in language* hard to understand.

Mystical intuition can also evolve, more creatively, into prophetic discourse. I would venture to suggest that legal discourse deals with things as they are. It takes the community as it is, with all its faults and foibles and tendency toward selfishness and injustice. But as soon as we manage to articulate things as they are, and write some laws governing outcomes, we begin to agitate for *how things could be*—better or different. I think that this evolutionary process—destabilized repeatedly by the dreamers and visionaries of the community—repeats itself over and over in the history of nations and curriculum committees.

To pursue the biblical illustration, let us follow the progression between a text from Deuteronomy, which articulates the laws of fasting, and another one from Isaiah, which asks the community to engage in a higher kind of fasting.

Here's Deuteronomy:

> Do not eat any food which brings defilement. You may eat such beasts as the ox, the sheep and the goat, red deer and roe, gazelle and wild goat, addax and orynx and zemer. (14:3–8)

—whatever a zemer is, and so on. Lots of good recipes.
Here's Isaiah:

> This is the fasting that I wish: releasing those bound unjustly; set-
> ting free the oppressed; breaking every yoke, sharing your bread
> with the hungry, sheltering the homeless, clothing the naked, not
> turning your back on your own. (Isaiah 58:6–7)

So law deals with *what is*, and what you can have for dinner,
and prophecy deals with *what could be*.

The ceramic artist, David Pye, in a book called *The Nature
and Art of Workmanship*, makes a similar distinction between
what he calls *workmanship of certainty* and *workmanship of risk*
(1999, 6–7). The former, like legal discourses, are works of
craft that have their outcome predetermined by tradition and
received wisdom, at an extreme by machine production, tool,
and dye. Workmanship of risk, by contrast, bears the mark of
the individual potter's thumb. Its outcome is dependent on the
crafter's judgment and skill, as well as on the uncontrollable
mystery of the fire. If we carry this distinction into the English
classroom, we might say that certain compositional forms
elicit workmanship of certainty, while others—notably what's
lumped together as expressivist pedagogies—constitute discourses "of risk."

I get emails from high school teachers all over the country
asking me why their school boards react with such fury to the
concept of "process writing." Well, because, personal writing
tends to privilege the prophetic voice. School boards and other
forces of legitimate social control have to be wary of calls to
higher ground; that's their job in community, being wary,
being obstructionist. The Isaiahan injunctions entrain a series
of delicate discriminations bureaucrats hate to make: about
who might be bound unjustly, *how much* bread is enough,
whose bed the poor are going to sleep in. This analysis should
certainly be in somebody's job description, but we shouldn't be
surprised if the school board wants to give it a pass.

What I've been trying to do here is simply make a few distinctions among the languages we hold in tension in the classroom and in our academic communities, perhaps without knowing that we do so. (As one of my advisees recently blurted, "It's English. It's my language. How hard can it be?") At this point, I feel rather like the crazy logician in Ionesco's play *Rhinoceros*, who worries more about how to pose the question than about how to deal with its implications: Have we seen "on two occasions a single rhinoceros bearing a single horn" or "on two occasions a single rhinoceros with two horns" or "an initial rhinoceros with two horns followed by a second with two horns" (1960, 35)?—when the real question, posed by common humanity in the play is, "But are we going to stand for our cats being run down under our very eyes by one-horned rhinoceroses or two . . . " (37)?

Here, I think, are the implications: Behind all this taxonomy, our cats are being run over. How can we listen to our texts and what space can we create for them to be heard? How do we attend to the stammer of student or colleague, and call it into analysis, description, argument, persuasion, or prophecy? How do we read tenure and promotion documents and listen to each other in the halls?

A few years ago at CCCCs, some of us arranged a panel on "Boredom, Burnout and Breakdown." At the end of what turned out to be a pretty contentious hour, a woman got up and spoke out, testified, I'm tempted to say. The tremor in her voice told us that it wasn't easy for her to do. "It's so hard to get into grad school," she said, "so hard to get a Ph.D., so hard to get a job and tenure. Then if we're very good—" here her voice went to the edge, "*they make us do it all our lives!*"

I keep telling this story to people, the story of what seemed a prophetic moment. It called into question things as they are and implicitly called the community to something better. Often when I tell people about this incident, I get a legalistic response, "Did she say '*let* us do it all our lives' or '*make* us do it all our lives?'" Which gulag are we in—modernist or po-mo? capitalist or fascist? Was she being ironic or literal? One horn or two?

For my part, I heard, "let." I heard irony. But it doesn't really matter. On the whole I think we have been conned rather than coerced into surrendering our freedom. We have bought in, attached ourselves as Thoreau would say, with our own "golden or silver fetters" (1986, 59). Or maybe it does matter whether we have been coerced or we have surrendered, because slavery is harder to get out of. I *think*.

What continues to interest me is the response this woman got. Or rather the nonresponse. I, for my part, said nothing to her, though clearly I pondered her words. Later it seemed to me that her exclamation was one of the two or three most important things said at CCCCs that year, and it was a good conference.

"A Voice Heard in Ramah": Mourning in Class

Ultimately, breakdown is a call to prophetic witness, and my contention is, again, that spiritual practice keeps the muscles toned to endure the inconvenience of working for social change.

I'm going to go right into the belly of the beast here, exploring a subject that all of us have had to learn a lot about since September 11: being with our students—and being with ourselves—in time of tragedy. I expect most readers will be familiar with the reference suggested in my heading: "A voice was heard in Ramah, weeping and gnashing of teeth, Rachel lamenting for her children, and will not be comforted because they are not" (Matthew 2:18).

My life as a teacher has been bracketed by the deaths of two students. In a long career, sadly, such losses are common: high school teachers in certain rough neighborhoods may lose two a year. But these particular deaths harrowed me, shifted my perspective, and taught me things that I want to bring forward at the moment. My general thesis about mourning in class is twofold—that, on the one hand, literature can serve a kind of liturgical function, a way that students can be helped to rise above the personal; on the other hand—as our colleagues in the more disciplined disciplines like to remind us—literature is all about the personal. Usually they mean this as an insult, but I'd like to suggest that our entanglement in messy, daily life can be a very good thing. There are always two ends of the church occupied at any good Irish funeral: the sanctuary, where the mourners try to get to some impersonal common ground, and the room where you keen and wail, pass around the Jamison's, and foment revolution.

Annette Flowers died the semester after I taught her as a freshman, my own first year of university teaching. She was what we'd now call a "nontraditional student," older than I. The company she worked for was paying her way through a business degree, and they weren't very happy about the fact that we were asking Annette to take literature courses. They wanted her to cut right to the accounting. In the course of the class, she began as the dutiful bookkeeper, making notes on the plot and reciting conscientiously.

Then English class became a place in which she began to act out a kind of spiritual quest. (Now that I think about it, this may be the primary motivator for most of our majors and serious students. Perhaps the fact that we have any majors at all, given the state of the job market, suggests the persistent intensity of spiritual longing in the human soul.) Annette started to invite me over to her house for dinner. She taught me to make that green bean dish with the kind of fried onions that come in a can. We would have long conversations over food like this about how metaphors work and how poems interrogate our lives.

Second semester, she came into my office with red lines painted on her skin where the doctors were aiming radiation; she had been diagnosed with lung cancer. Literature had now become her passion. She—and her husband—were rereading the books from English 101. It's not currently fashionable to look to literature for meaning, but stay tuned. It could be the next fad. She and I talked a lot about how Willie Loman had lived his life, what choices he made, what went wrong with his kids. We were using literature, that is, as a public enactment of an inner search, probing matters perhaps too delicate to be brought into another kind of conversation.

There's a piece of statuary on our campus that carries the inscription, "In the beginning was the word." Those of you who have heard of Ramah probably recognize this sentence as the beginning of John's Gospel, *en arche hein ho logos*. For some reason, when I was taking second-year Greek (a contentious young agnostic at the time), I became obsessed with figuring out this text—as did my Jewish friend, Stephen, who went on to become a poet—both of us trying to grasp the nature of this errant scrap of language floating across the threshold of time. One of my scholarly friends tells me that the Greek word *logos* carries a freight of Hellenistic association. We might, he says, translate the gospel concept as "In the beginning was the promise of meaning." In the beginning was the promise that you are not lost forever in the Forest of Derrida.

Students need to know this. I need to know this. After Annette died, I started asking an extra question of myself as I prepared my yearly syllabus, along with, Does it include works that reflect gender issues and racial and ethnic diversity? *Will it help us to die well?*

The second death occurred in the spring of 2002. A Latin American student I'll call Diego Vargas hung himself in his dorm room. The class Diego took with me was a special one, taught under a Contemplative Fellowship Grant from the American Council for Learned Societies. There were only eight students. We met in an upper room of the campus ministry house, sat on the floor, and began class with fifteen minutes of centering prayer or Zen meditation. We read our texts slowly and often aloud, like medieval monks. We got so attached to each other that we'd meet on weekends in coffee houses around town to practice writing together. Dads and moms and significant others got dragged in; several unregistered students were reported to be eavesdropping from the next room. We'd all get to class early and have tea in the kitchen and stay late talking about literature. Perhaps every teacher longs for the conditions that will allow her to teach her dream class; this was mine. And yet such a terrible thing happened.

Diego was, bluntly, our pet. He was a political refugee from a repressive regime, a little older than the rest, smart and funny, and a brilliant writer. Also, he was asthmatic and frequently ill. "I miss my *abuelita* so much," he wheezed one day. "We will be your *abuelita*," I told him. We made him ginger tea and let him lie on the floor. He seemed to be thriving on the issues of the course. He told me one day, "You know, since your class, I feel so alive."

I later discovered that Diego had had, as the social workers call it, a suicidal ideation since being tortured in prison. Sometimes all we can do is keep someone in life a little longer. Who knows what the connections are among us and what each is helping the other to do? One of the students in that class wrote a letter to Diego later: *"You were my older brother trying to wake me up . . . I refused to wake, but right after you stopped breathing you kicked your feet and struck me in the side."*

We began that class as a friendly group, we ended in almost familial bonding. Those students knew where I keep my door key, the habits of my dog; four students, at one point, had slept over. I'm a person who likes to make a little separation between home and school, but, as we all know, when one member of a community commits suicide, the rest are uniquely at risk. Opening my home to these students certainly stretched me. And at my age, I'm kind of like an old rubberband, once I'm stretched, I'm stretched forever.

Grief politicized us, as well. The voice heard in Ramah has to cry loudly enough for the administrators to hear. We had a series of meetings with campus authorities about providing support for students who are victims of political oppression. There are many more "displaced persons" on our campuses than anyone suspects. A couple of years ago I got caught up in the Midwestern misadventures of a student who had seen his whole family murdered in Rwanda. One thing I discovered in dealing with such students is that it's often when the student feels himself to be safe that the nightmares and flashbacks and survivor's guilt start in. At about the time he winds up in English 101.

So what would a pedagogy of grief looked like? We cried in class. We made a rule, *Cry and keep talking. Cry and keep writing.* We didn't want the whole class to be about the tragedy, but we didn't want to leave our friend behind, either. As the course progressed, we had to confront a strange revelation: that each of us, individually, was struggling to find a version he could live with, or which would let us live. Earlier, I said that such versioning tends to feed the ego's perspective; but I also noted that it is a salvific process, subject to more nuanced revision when one is older and braver. In the beginning was the possibility of meaning: to teach from this principle is, as Buddhists say, right livelihood.

The pressure of death made everything important, *alive.* Diego had written this: "Your blood, humans, has to carry along your trees and your sunsets and your rivers and your buildings and your cars and your books and the names of those who you love and the names of those who you will love . . . and the day you lost your first tooth and the day you kissed for the very first time and the few days you sat under the apple or orange or banana or *vaya-usted-asaber-cual-fruta* tree and saw that star and laughed because you knew it was yours and yours only. Is your soul that cheap that you have forgotten these random acts of happiness?"

We said, *No.* Students in that class—let me just list their activities here—went to Washington to protest the School of the Americas, dialogued with the local hydroelectric about violation of native treaty rights, labored with the physical plant about pesticide use on campus, spearheaded a diversity teach-in to plead the cause of Muslim students, and hatched a plan to turn an abandoned green house into a sustainability center/coffee shop that would sell free trade coffee. They got involved in an alliance for gay, lesbian, bisexual, and transgendred (GLBT) students on campus. They founded a meditation group that still meets on Thursday afternoons. One boy went off to a monastery the next semester. Two others spent the next year teaching in inner-city schools.

For, in retrospect, the course *was* about Diego. Or it was about the shadow subject, death, which, make no mistake, is always sitting in the corner of our classrooms. And therefore it was about the choice for life. I think it always is.

Why a pedagogy of grief? If we welcome a prophetic discourse into our classrooms and communities we will quickly learn that prophecy—and consequently social change—originate in a peculiar crucible of contemplation, mourning and what—with apologies to Thich Nhat Hanh—I shall cautiously name *holy rage* (in the midst of which one can still pray, or rearrange the flowers). Walter Bruggemann writes: "I believe that the proper idiom for the prophet in cutting through [authoritarian] numbness and denial is the *language of grief*, the rhetoric that engages the community in mourning for a funeral they do not want to admit. It is indeed their own funeral" (1981, 50).

Chapter 4

Sustainable Teaching

Let Them Not Make Me a Stone

*W*hat would sustainable teaching look like? Might it be possible to establish a practice that we can return to September after September with a sense of anticipation and even exuberance?

When I wrote *The Peaceable Classroom* in 1984, I quoted at length from Archibald MacLeish's poem, "Prayer Before Birth" with its resonant conclusion: "Let them not make me a stone and let them not spill me. . . ." At the time, this poem articulated for me the wordless longing of students for real, not phony, life, as well as the innocence with which they put themselves into our hands. Now, in the grandmotherly stage of my career, I am likely to quote this poem in support of young teachers, who enter our profession with such idealism and passion.

Don't become a monk, traditional Zen teachers used to say, making aspirants wait outside the gate through snowfall and sunstroke.

Don't become a teacher.

Don't become a nurse.

Don't become a social worker.

Don't enter what are so cosily called the *helping professions.* Why, against my advice, do my students—and even my children, godchildren, and nieces—keep wanting to do this: help? One of my former students drops by to tell me he's leaving his well-paid position in Internet security to become a high school music teacher.

I warn him off. "I'd like to make you sit out in the alley for a year, like those Japanese abbots, before I let you in."

He prepares to sit. "Now I know your secret. *There is something in there.*"

Well, you're the security expert. There *is* something in there, but to be happy at it you need strong practice. Sitting in the alley is better preparation than an education degree, what used to be called Normal School. Try Abnormal School.

Many aspects of life in the helping professions are beyond our control—though not beyond our agitation for change—and we have to anticipate, each day, a level of incoherence. I'm not paranoid enough to blame the government or the school board for consciously trying to make our lives miserable, but I know that frontline soldiers in the helping wars deal with a daily muddle, much of it originating with people who are supposed to be supporting our work although they themselves have little sense of what it means to *do* it. I have no hopes for unraveling this set of knots in my lifetime, but I must warn young teachers that what issues forth from "above" will be confusing, destabilizing, shame-inducing, and usually unfair.

Work is best approached in a certain coyote spirit. Obedience is not the virtue that is going to make anyone the most happy or effective teacher. Our system breaks the obedient and good. Outright disobedience, I suppose, will end your career abruptly. In between, one might perfect the discipline of affability, whilst declining to do a single thing that doesn't make sense to you or that you don't find to be for the good of your students. Since we all have more to do than we can possibly get through, what's meaningless to you can usually be stricken off the to-do list. You owe it to your own precious life not to be made into a stone, not to be spilled.

It may help to realize that we in education, health, and social services are frequently asked to make bricks without straw. I often meet teachers shopping at the Goodwill store who are carting in their own straw, buying the supplies for underfunded classrooms.

Be as Crazy as You Are

My friend Peter Crysdale says, "I can't be a pastor if I can't be as crazy as I am."

Neither can I be a teacher, at this stage of my life, if I can't be as crazy as I am.

My young colleague has just gotten a bad teaching review and a scolding from the head of her department. She leans over her cup of tea, eyes bright with tears. "He says I have to be tough, that the students ride all over me. And that's true. But I can't be tough. I can't act a part all day. It's so exhausting. . . . "

It does no good for us, as mentors, to tell quiet people to assert themselves or the prissy to loosen up, or the rigid to soften—though these accomodations may be, after the journey of a long career, the ones they need to make. We may see it, they may see it, but nobody can make it happen. Instead, we have to teach young professionals to negotiate small compromises between their identity and their jobs if they are to survive the tenuring process—for example, my colleague could post a syllabus that promises uncompromising rigor yet never raise her voice; she could borrow the ruthless language of Dr. Hardapple's feedback forms and not subvert her graceful poise.

Yet, to expand on a comment I made earlier, most of us have more freedom than we ever use, and the older we get the more inefficiently we squander our liberty. The best defense we can make for the peculiar institution of tenure is that it protects freedom of academic discourse; however, my astute colleague, Lon Otto, remarked many years ago that, "By the time people get tenure, they've already been co-opted." Although I am in what I optimistically think of as the last third of my teaching career, I have rarely taught in a way that feels entirely *authentic*—there's that word again—to me. Most of us teach under a set of covenants, written or simply understood, about the kinds of texts and methodologies we incorporate into our classroom practice. Such collegial understandings are good—

they are a variety of that legal discourse I tried to honor in Chapter 3—but they can impede a prophetic call for change.

I grew up in a variety of systems that respect tradition, and I, for my part, honor the structures that keep an overstimulated beginner from having to make up every move every day. Yet a delicate discernment has to take place at the point where an individual's inner guidance starts to chafe against institutional structure. To feel that point of friction is to be challenged to ponder our actions. In any communal venture, be it marriage or departmental life, we must ask *Am I being polished up or am I being ground down?* (This is another of Peter's queries.)

The quest to live out one's professional vision can be self-indulgent, misguided, or paradoxically, the recourse of an ego too fragile to submit to external oversight. The supporters of the status quo will happily put such constructions on every innovative gesture. Sometimes they are correct, but we should not hang back out of fear of self-assertion. One's individual vocation is lived out in community, for the good of the community. Thich Nhat Hanh teaches, "You sit for the world." We also *stand up* on behalf of the world. If you allow your prophetic vocation to be squashed out of fear, you are withdrawing your gifts from the community.

"You know," Peter told me, "you go around like a dog at the end of a chain for so long that when you get off the chain you hardly know where to run."

I have given twenty-five years to collegial discipline. Don't I owe five years to God—I ask myself. Or at least to Walt Whitman?

Get out of There

Sometimes, if there is nothing in the inferno that is not the inferno, you just have to get out of there, be it the room, the school, or the country.

Recently a professor of education invited me to speak to her class of perspective high school teachers. The professor had set up the group to offer me an alarming test case, which one student timidly brought forward: "What do you do when you are put in charge of a class that's too large, when the students are completely unruly, when you have no supplies, no support [etc.]?"

I guess the professor expected me to problem-solve this one, but I just said, "You should throw as many shoes as you can into the machine, and then you should leave. You must not allow your life to be used up that way." Even Jesus sometimes told his disciples to get out of there, to shake the dust from their sandals.

The important thing is to leave with good heart. The case history these students presented to me is not so different from what I read in desperate emails from my students who've gone off to teach in some Fort Apache High School for board, room, and twelve credits in education. I *know* they will have to leave. I write their recommendations with a heavy heart and a generous pen. The best I hope for is that they will not leave with a sense of personal failure. Did the recreation director on the Titanic feel guilty because the guests had a bad day? I just hope she made it into a lifeboat.

I hope you will not leave teaching forever, but rather retire now and again to get your breath. Retreat, replenishment, nurturance—how quickly we can lose track of the importance of these simple requirements of the stable soul. These are my crisis queries: Are you eating properly? Are you exercising? Are you practicing your art? Are you involved with communities that love and honor and challenge you? Do you have someone to talk to about your life? *Are you being polished up or ground down?*

Be Wise as Serpents and Gentle as Doves

One of the reasons I look to Jesus as an example of good professional practice is that he was such a trickster. In Matthew 10:16, he told his teaching assistants, "Behold I send you forth as sheep in the midst of wolves. Be therefore wise as serpents and harmless as doves." As often as I read this text, it makes me laugh. Maybe it is one of those rabbi jokes that so often confuse our reading of the Christian Scriptures. Or perhaps it's a complicated koan. Sometimes I think that Jesus, a good yeshiva boy, only got out of the library to look for metaphors. When he starts on the subject of sheep, goats, and wildlife he often makes the farmers in the audience smile, as my students do when I grasp at sports metaphors.

Because I do volunteer work at a wildlife sanctuary, I see quite the selection of snakes, which I happen to be fond of. I find them to be gentle creatures, except when they have their eye on dinner, which is also true of you or me. And I think that the most dedicated herpetologist will admit that snakes, though they have a mythic reputation for cunning, are about as clever as a two-by-four.

We also see a lot of doves in rehabilitation—rock doves, specifically. Our common Minnesota rock dove is not the most poetic species of bird. I'm sure the Holy Ghost did not descend in the form of a husky pigeon. But rock doves are *very* smart. They are not harmless. A nesting pair tore a big hole in my roof, not once but three times, and not even the Allstate agent could figure out what was going on. They are sneaky little flying rats, working away under the eaves.

What, then, is the point of this mixed-up koan, with its confusing menage of animal life? It certainly reminds us that there are two complicated ways of being in the world—soft and gentle, on the one hand, and, on the other, canny, analytic, and hard-nosed. Skillful action in the classroom requires both modalities. But, examined closely, the scriptural story has a chaotic center: be wise, be gentle, *whatever*. Things are still going to get out of hand. Expect a world that's inverted, disguised, deconstructed, and full of whatever masquerading animal you least expect. What should I do? Whatever you're best at. When I was raising sheep, I got good results by speaking softly and holding still; my coshepherd got good results by kicking them in the tail. Perhaps the message of this parable or koan is simply, *Prepare for chaos. Be a moving target. Don't get head-butted.*

As I smile at this antic zoology, I return to Mike Heller's advice that we ponder the foundational metaphors that inform our sense of departmental community. In an earlier chapter, I fastened on the lifeboat. It will be no surprise to anyone who knows me if I fetch up, in conclusion, on another image, one which has formed so much of my thinking about the teaching profession, Elias Hicks' Peaceable Kingdom.

When I started writing about this painting, I had a particular version of it before my eyes. I did not know, then, that Elias Hicks was (like me) obsessed with his text from Isaiah, and painted its story over and over at various stages of his life—as I suppose I am doing also. A few years ago, all of these paintings were brought together in a touring exhibit, and I went to see them. What surprised me was how often and how radically the painter shifted the focus of his allegory. Elias Hicks himself lived a long, contentious life, and he was a big critter in a small community. He painted his first lion as young and svelte; later, the beast became crafty-looking. But at this stage of my life it is the aged lion that draws my attention: he is vacant, disheveled, and obviously on his last legs. This lion will lie down with the lamb because the lion is toothless and exhausted. He has become, of necessity, a vegetarian.

I'm not going to teach until I look like that ragged lion. In terms of role models, I'm shooting for something more like the Velveteen Rabbit, though deconstructionists might decry the goal of becoming Real.

The Trial of Idealism

When I worry about the abuse of innocence that young faculty often suffer, I'm particularly aware of the experience of teachers in small denominational colleges because most of my work has been done in such contexts—not only as a teacher, but as the kind of consultant whose job is to "hear the cries of the people," like (in that respect alone) the bodhisatva Kuan-Yin. But what I have to say about the small-college ambience will certainly apply to anyone who comes to college teaching with an ideal of service in mind.

People do not necessarily accept teaching positions at religious colleges for religious reasons. The job market being what it is, there are people who will take any job that's offered them—perhaps even *convert*, if that is the issue, to whatever ideology offers them four sections of freshmen something per semester and a living wage, be it to Hadisic Judaism or snake-handling. But at most religious institutions and small liberal arts colleges, a delicate process of mutual discernment goes on. Where I teach, we call it The Question, one that's asked of our candidates from the initial interview through the dean's interrogation at the campus visit: *What do you feel you have to offer to a Catholic teaching institution?*

We debate a candidate's answers to this question with the avidity we bring to any textual analysis. At one time, twenty years ago, there was a perfect answer to The Question: "I'm a Catholic, and I hope to attend daily Mass with my students." This was the best answer—not the only answer that would get you the job—certainly it was not the one I was able to give. But it was an answer that ensured clear sailing, on that point at least, through constituencies as disparate as the English department and the Board of Trustees.

Nowadays I doubt we would ever hear this answer or particularly welcome it if we did. We don't expect our candidates to be Christian, even: but we do look for a kind of *fit*. It certainly doesn't hurt if a young professor knows something about how religious institutions, or small colleges, work in contrast to large universities. We want new colleagues to know that they will have lots of student contact, that undergraduate teaching will be very important, and that the kind of professional engagement expected of them may be less rigorously quantifiable than that required at a public university. Service will loom large, both to the university and in terms of leadership with students; our faculty may as likely be found teaming up with their students to tutor in a disadvantaged grade school as at a professional conference. The Question, as it's articulated today, codes an understanding that a heavy courseload may make it difficult to achieve the level of national visibility professors get at first-tier research institutions, or the salary, or the research assistance, or the sabbaticals. We want incoming faculty to understand these tradeoffs—although as I articulate them, I have to wonder what we're trading *for*—we want them to be with us in our mission of teaching and service.

I'm explaining our discernment process, as I understand it, in some detail, because I think it's a template for what goes on at most small institutions. Some may be more doctrinally focused—requiring, even, a signed loyalty oath to fundamental orthodoxies; others may require little more than a nod to foundational principles.

People, in my experience, come to teach at religious colleges for the same complicated reasons they go to church. Prominent among these reasons is, of course, faith in the enterprise, its ideology, and its proposed outcomes. But there are other reasons as well, which do not always rise to the level of intentionality—the desire, perhaps, to belong to a family or community. Often young aspirants come out of a small, intact communal center, church, town, and school. Their formative experiences originate in healthy community or family. It's hard for such people to imagine a different educational context and they are drawn to re-create it. While—especially in today's market—these young faculty may be fully competitive in the first-tier market, they return to a small liberal arts denominational college out of what they may call a sense of vocation. By and large, such people do well in their chosen contexts; expectations seem to create the desired results. They may relate well to the idea of the St. Trinian's Family; they may publish little and accept low wages as a contribution to some higher purpose. In the old days, such individuals retired honorably to putter in their gardens and in the fullness of time were buried from the college chapel.

A different kind of young person comes to religion—or to the denominational college—as the product of a more fragmented world. They may come out of longing for families and pieties they never experienced. They may carry a brokenness that makes them vulnerable to the peculiar stresses of small-college life, worst of all, may be the implicit fear of being rejected by yet another community.

In truth, we are probably all a product of mixed motivations in our choice of a teaching career—venal, idealistic, and wounded—and to the extent we are innocent about the nature of ourselves and the world we will be vulnerable to the peculiar stresses of academic life, be it at a large university or a small prairie college. The more predatory administrators and colleagues intuitively recognize an aspirant's capacity to be punished, mocked, overlooked, ignored, insulted, and scapegoated. What better reason to give him tenure?

Thus, one may become embittered.

Do I seem to overstate the cruelties of academic life? I have sat in on administrative meetings where promulgations like this one went unchallenged: "Our faculty are like tubes of toothpaste, you can always get more out of them." I have seen a widow laid off at the reception following her husband's funeral. Here's a story with a happier ending: I knew one elderly female faculty member who refused to enter into a lawsuit when other women in her department discovered that they had been paid a discriminatory wage; "Why, it might bankrupt St. Trinian's to repay me after all these years," she told me affably. Then the college fired her. She responded by negotiating for the college press to publish her book of poetry. The press agreed, expecting some harmless collection of maidenly lyrics. It turned out to be a racy collection of erotica.

It's hard to live up to one's scholarly potential at the kind of institution I'm talking about. Certain colleges seem to breed a conspiracy of mediocrity similar to the understandings formed among those jocks with the baseball caps leaning against the wall in English 101. An individual who does publish may be denigrated for a lapse in team spirit. Innumerable young poets have lamented to me that colleagues ignore their awards, publications, and readings, as though such achievements let down the side. One young scholar remarked that, when she came back from a year on a prestigious fellowship, her office mate joked that he thought she had been away in a mental institution. I once drove across the plains with an earnest scholar who was weeping because his dean had just told him, "Whenever I see your name in print I see a teacher who's neglecting his students." This professor's life work happened to be a biography of the founder of his religious order, but from the administrative perspective it might well have been Mr. Casaubon's Unified Theory of All Religion. He cried for a long time. I got a little worried because he was driving, but he seemed to be handling it.

It follows that the person who thrives best at a small denominational college is the one who has her need for communal acceptance under control, who is realistically aware of the limits of institutional benevolence, who prioritizes her scholarly agenda, and who is willing to seek a professional community outside the cloistering walls of the department. A canny prof once said to me, "Whenever I hear the phrase 'St. Trinian's family' I go for my gun."

This is the world we have *to practice*. Be wise, be gentle: there is an intractable mystery at the center of it that will yield predictably to neither approach. Yet I have called the academic department "a school for love," and it has provided me with the curriculum I've needed, though not one I can pretend, yet, to have passed.

Teachers who share a fundamental orientation to service—whether in the small college or the state university—differ in a wide range of respects, but they seem to have one quality in common: the suspicion, at least, that materialism cannot sustain their happiness. They live in what Lewis Hyde, in his book *The Gift*, distinguishes as an economy of blessing rather than an economy of entitlement.

Hyde tells the story about a Polynesian tribe that had the habit of exchanging shell necklaces as a way of honoring grand occasions or gifting a great leader. When they tried this hospitality on visiting Englishmen, however, they got a nasty surprise: the Englishman would get back in his boat and tear away, much to the consternation of the indigenous people. It took a long time for the English to catch on that when a chief bestowed a necklace upon a neighboring chief, the neighbor did not *keep* them, but distributed the shells all over his island. When the observers returned a year later, everyone in the tribe would have one of those shells.

There was, then, among people formerly called *primitive*, an economy in which blessings circulate; white Europeans, by contrast, saw the world as a place to pile up toys, the more you had the better. Clearly the man with the most toys was the most powerful; whilst in many tribal cultures, status was measured by what you could give away.

People who choose the economy of blessing make themselves vulnerable to all sorts of abuse of which the worst is disillusionment. We need to prize our gifts and not let them be squandered. The Islamic proverb puts it this way: "Trust in God, but tie your camel to a tree." Here you are in Tahiti or wherever, giving away all your cowrie shells while the English sailors keep theirs, corner the market, and sell them back to you at a high rate of exchange. If you live in the economy of gift, beware of people who don't play by your rules. *Behold I send you out as sheep among wolves.*

Yet it's more fun to pass on blessings than to hoard and whine. It's simply more fun.

Psychologist Daniel Gilbert and his team at Harvard have, since the 1990s, been replicating experiments of Jesus, Socrates, and Henry David Thoreau: possessions don't make you happy. Harvard found that we *know* this, but have a kind of amnesia about the fact. A certain low level of stuff makes us happy—indoor plumbing makes us happy, a few cowrie shells and say, cable TV, whatever. But beyond that, the Harvard study suggests, we have poor imagination for what's going to give us satisfaction and we forget what didn't make us happy last time we overextended our credit card for the Porshe or the fur-covered toilet seat.

Still in School

Thinking through issues for the book that became *The Peaceable Classroom* some fifteen years ago, I wrote a sentence that took me to the edge of my courage as a teacher: "What we learn is more important than what they learn." This is—or so it seemed to me—a frightening concept for the dutiful, self-sacrificing professional. However, since I try to write every day after meditation or some artistic work that takes me on a visit to the unconscious, I am obligated to receive my journal entries as least as attentively and hospitably as I might a puzzling dream that wakens me at 3 A.M. I had to think that sentence through.

What our students learn is the focus of our lives as teachers: how could it not be paramount? And yet we control so little, really, of what our students learn. They hear things exactly backward (a phenomenon of brain wiring every teacher has surely pondered as she checks journals or class notes). They hear what reinforces their preconceptions. They absorb mysterious time-release capsules that determine some consequential action, its antecedents utterly obscure, twenty years in the future. What I think they learn, above all, is a kind of gut sense, rather like that of fishes swimming in what's so appropriately called a *school*, about the pulsing organism of class life. The class has a collective being, of which the teacher may or may not even be the brain, and in this spirit-body things happen, things we call learning.

But, again, *we* are the ones who have stayed in school, trapped forever like flies in the amber of our youth. I used to ask myself repeatedly in the classroom, *What did I just teach?* I was trying to alert myself to issues of process rather than to issues of content. For example, I catch myself teaching people to be snots, and to doubt their hearts; introducing them to the jargon of graduate studies in literature, I subtly inculcate the idea that things they previously trusted as dependable resources are mere "constructions"; I teach them over and over that I am competent and they are not.

Fortunately, I control very little of what they learn.

I found it more painful to ask myself, by way of experiment, *What did I just learn?* Learning is harder work than teaching. I have to examine my resistance, my unwillingness to shift the boundaries of what I think is true about the world. I understand why my students sometimes look so exhausted and cynical. Let me at those course evaluations! This class is too hard. The teacher is incompetent. We are all adrift and the wind is rising.

What we learn is more important than what they learn. In retrospect, I stand by this edgy sentence because my own life is the only one I can answer for. In the helping professions, much of our time is spent devising ways to give other people what we have determined they need. We can't do this, day after day, without acquiring a little smile about the absurdity of the proposition. If we lose our sense of humility we become intolerable fascists. More important, we close off our options for growth and change. Shunryo Suzuki titled his classic analysis *Zen Mind, Beginner's Mind*, with the recognition that opening, always, to infinite possibility is the foundation of stable practice. This is paradoxical, because we think that limited choices—orthodoxies of one kind or another—provide structure. And they do. But when they become security addictions, they limit our freedom.

I think that the experience of Dark Night inevitably comes to teach us more and more about who we are and what might be the nature of the world we inhabit: *What did I just learn?* Darkness interrogates us at the places where our knowledge of reality is most deficient, our illusions most entrenched and intractable. To be stuck this way is called, in most wisdom traditions, *attachment*. The Dark Night is essentially a trial of innocence, that quality so charming in the young and so appalling when it persists into adulthood, which is not, in that case, maturity. One danger of the Dark Night is that we will fail its test, but let's put aside our academic perfectionism for the moment. We will inevitably fail such tests and the universe in its wisdom will simply send it back without a grade.

We cling to innocence because it shelters us in an idea of ourselves or the world that makes us feel safe and valuable. At the root of this clinging is the terrible fear that we are *not* safe and valuable. You might as well let that go—get into the millrace and discover that despite the oddity of one's unique vocation and despite the instability of our communities, *we are safe and valuable*. None of us wants to jump off the dock into the tumultuous water where we learn things, and so the experience of Dark Night comes along to give us a push.

The great test of this time is to maintain an open heart, not to close in cynicism and self-protection. At least not permanently. If you are given to prayer or aligning your life to the purposes of the universe, the best and perhaps the only utterance one is capable of at such a time is the prayer that one's heart be opened, one's compassion increased. My daughter, in her first years of professional life, remarked to me, "I have discovered that the prayer for a compassionate heart is always answered, and that I am never going to like the process."

For opening the heart, Buddhism gives us the discipline of *metta*. Let me tell you about how I failed at this simple practice, which my spiritual director taught to me in the midst of a professional crisis. *Metta* is a Sanskrit word that means "blessing" or "merit." In metta practice, you learn to bless, first, yourself, then those you love, and finally those you perceive to be enemies. In the form I was taught, one begins by repeating a series of blessings for oneself: "May I be safe, may my body be well, may my mind be at peace, may I find my true path and rest in the light." Then you repeat this series of prayers for someone you love dearly—this is the easiest part for most of us. Next you repeat it, concentrating on someone you feel neutral about; finally you bless your enemy. In committing to this practice, I think we learn to focus our compassionate attention. It's easy to bless one's self or one's child, and that blessing becomes a lens through which we learn to focus compassion for a wider community.

But, as noted, I failed.

After a few months of metta practice I went wailing back to my teacher. I could *not* bless those who had dealt me wounds that felt mortal, I could *not* pray for their physical, emotional, and spiritual security. While I didn't want them to break out in boils, I was hoping for a temporary rash. I wanted their minds to be at best a little unquiet. Metta practice felt—worst sin to a child of the sixties—inauthentic.

My teacher let out a snort of laughter. "I suppose you are rattling through the whole thing at once, the way you always do. Eating the whole pie?"

"Did I get it wrong?"

"Why don't you just stick to the first part? Pray for yourself for a year. Maybe ten. Then go on to the rest."

So here I am, still in metta kindergarten. "My own heart let me more have pity on . . . " (1963, 63)—Gerard Manley Hopkins, no slouch at negotiating the Dark Night, learned to exclaim.

Is there then no release? Are we stuck here forever, between trains, whining interminably? Not in my experience, which is all I can speak about. I have mentioned a loss of innocence; another way to say the same thing is that the paradigm, the structure of meaning we have been sheltering in, is revealed to be too small. Being born into a new, broader existence hurts, and when we are in transition we are as vulnerable as a soft-shell crab, but once we have made the passage we find that we like the new landscape well enough. And I think that in this transition compassion is inevitably born. We can look back and see that the one we imagine to be an enemy—given the sea she was swimming in and the shell that armored her—did the best she could. And negotiating the process (over and over) has given me an acute sense of how important it is to support young people as they, with so much pain, lose their innocent view of self and community. Which is simply to say, I have been learning to do my job, and for most graduate degrees in education, we expect to pay tuition.

Sometimes, as Martin Luther argued, we get a grant.

Take a Nap

Grace comes to us through suffering and through rest. I prefer the latter.

The idea of spirituality is frequently conjoined with *relaxation* these days. People take up yoga or meditation in order to experience peace and serenity, relief from physical and mental distress. Actually, I can't think of any other reason to stand on my head. Americans are oriented to the payoff.

People flock to retreat centers to get away from their kids and husbands and greedy golden retrievers. A sound bite on National Public Radio recently told of this "latest fix for the frenzied soul": the chance to spend a weekend praying the liturgy of the hours and meeting with a monastic spiritual director. They also interviewed a nun who offered massage therapy at her retreat center, and, if memory serves me right, those nuns had a hot tub on the place. A few years ago I was offered a job doing what they called spiritual counseling at the classiest spa in the midwest, a place better known for its heated mineral pools and mint-leaf body wraps. People, women especially, are bombarded with advertising that commingles the spiritual and the sybaritic, the come-on inevitably phrased with some version of "Take the time for Capital-You," as if we weren't, women included, the most self-obsessed race of people who ever crawled out of a thermal mud bath.

So what? That's where we begin.

Some of our conflation of spirituality and vacationing becomes apparent when we try to pin down the meaning of the word *spirituality*, or to distinguish it from religion. I used to say, with a certain sneer, that spirituality was religion without the bother and inconvenience. I was tough-minded when I was young. Now I'm arthritic and need a mint body wrap. As it turns out, I've never been able to make a distinction between religion and spirituality that satisfied me. Religion tends to be tied to institutional identifications, while spirituality is a more free-floating term; Karl Jung remarked that religion is what society sets up to protect us from spirituality, and there's a lot to chew on in that remark, but on the whole I've given up the enterprise of definition.

What's clear to me, however, is that religion and spirituality address our experience of suffering and surrender, the latter being another, and more spiritual, word for *napping*.

Sometimes people come to me with a kind of wistful plea, "I'd like to have a spiritual life." I shudder for them because I know they have uttered a kind of prayer. They have asked for admission to a first-tier educational establishment, and I anticipate that pretty soon something painful is going to happen to them. "I would like to learn . . . " they say, and the universe responds, "Well, here is something to practice on." It's like saying "I kind of wish I could play the violin"; then the teacher hands you a delicate instrument and you have to play a lot of scales.

But I don't want to pour any more holy water on the idea of suffering. The universe will hand you a violin once in a while, whether or not you pray. Let's be practical. The Dalai Lama, who is so rational in his analysis of the spiritual life, typically puts it this way: "You can be bitter and mean-spirited, jealous, you can think of yourself as a victim, if you want to, but does that really make you happy? Wouldn't it be better to examine what states of mind bring you peace and tranquility and cultivate them?"

Since pain will come to us anyway, why not figure out how to deal with it? It's hard to grasp the connection between suffering and spiritual growth if we think of spiritual practice only as a way to gain peace and tranquility. To recall one of the songs of my youth: "I don't care if it rains or freezes, 'long as I got my Plastic Jesus" (from *Plastic Jesus* by Ernie Marrs).

This is not the wisdom of the great spiritual songs and stories; this is not the wisdom of "Amazing Grace" or the Diamond Sutra. Even by the most mundane standards of progress, spiritual practice will seem to get you almost nowhere. I had a brief and succinct conversation recently with my seat mate on a transatlantic flight, a middle-aged man with shaven head and sandals who gives lectures all over the world in a yogic discipline. He was having a bad day on the spiritual circuit. "I wish I had never met my teacher," he told me. "I wish I was still a businessman. I wish I had never found the path. It's all a big pain in the butt."

I had to agree. "But," I said, "speaking just for myself, if I hadn't I would be nuts by now."

"Oh sure, me too," he grumped.

So, ultimately, the conflation of relaxation and religion doesn't bother me. Things are tough, and not only on transatlantic flights. The angels love to find people while they are sleeping, deep in their dreams. I read this in the Bible. I think the angels like to find us any place we can't reach the cell phone, because the relentless overstimulation of the modern work environment is probably our greatest barrier to experiencing transcendence. Work is, in today's world, what traditional spiritual teachers used to call the "mammon of iniquity": we render to it a power and authority in our lives that should be reserved for that which is most holy. I love the lines of the Islamic poet Hafiz (1999, 183), which I always take with me on retreat and contemplate in my mint body wrap:

> Just sit there right now
> Don't do a thing
> Just rest.

For your separation from God,
From love,

Is the hardest work
In this
World.

Epilogue: Cucumbers

My goals in writing this book have been modest. If I have given the reader a sense of being less lonely, I will have succeeded. In writing honestly about my life—the only one I know—I always come to a quandary. One of my editors once said of a manuscript I'd turned in, which happened to be about farming, "Something has to happen at the end. You have to come to some kind of new understanding. Or there has to be some dramatic finish."

But, I had to respond, *I couldn't manage to get killed by a tractor.*

I think that the crises of professional life always propel us toward greater freedom, though the nature of that freedom depends on the kind of attachments each of us struggles with. Thus I hesitate—no, I refuse—to orchestrate a vision of transcendence that would seem as phony as any other literary description of sunrise. You've all seen the sun rise, once or twice. One of my relatives, who drank a bit, once woke me up in the middle of the night to "look at the beautiful morning!" It turned out that she'd fallen asleep on the floor and left on the bathroom light. But I appreciated the wake-up call. It still makes me smile.

I'll just sit a moment in conclusion with Suzuki Roshi:

One thing flows into another and cannot be grasped. Before the rain stops we hear a bird. Even under the heavy snow we see snowdrops and some new growth. . . . In Japan in the spring we eat cucumbers. (138)

Works Cited

Beck, Charlotte Joko. 1993. *Nothing Special: Living Zen*. Edited by Steve Smith. San Francisco: Harper.

Berry, Wendell. 1981. "Solving for Pattern," in *The Gift of Good Land*, 134–35. San Francisco: North Point Press.

Bolt, Robert. 1962. *A Man for All Seasons*. New York: Vintage.

Bruggemann, Walter. 1981. *The Prophetic Imagination*. Philadelphia, PA: Fortress.

Calvino, Italo. 1972. *Invisible Cities*. Translated by William Weaver. New York: Harcourt Brace Jovanovich.

Chittister, Joan, O.S.B. 1990. *Wisdom Distilled from the Daily*. New York: Harper and Row.

Dillard, Annie. 1974. *Pilgrim at Tinker Creek*. San Francisco: Harper.

Doherty, Catherine de Hueck. 1975. *Poustinia: Christian Spirituality of the East and Western Man*. Notre Dame, IN: Ave Maria.

Doty, Mark. 1997. *Heaven's Coast*. New York: Harper Collins.

Fitzgerald, Constance. 1984. "Impasse and Dark Night." In *Living with Apocalypse: Spiritual Resources for Social Compassion*, edited by Tilden H. Edwards. San Francisco: Harper and Row.

Hafiz. 1999. "A Cushion for Your Head." In *The Gift: Poems by Hafiz, the Great Sufi Master*. Translated by Daniel Ladinsky. New York: Penguin.

Hopkins, Gerard Manley. 1963. *Poems and Prose of Gerard Manley Hopkins*. London: Penguin.

Hyde, Lewis. 1983. *The Gift: Imagination and the Erotic Life of Property*. New York: Random House.

Illian, Clary. 1999. *A Potter's Workbook*. Iowa City: University of Iowa Press.

Ionesco, Eugene. 1960. *Rhinoceros and Other Plays*. Translated by Derek Prouse. New York: Grove.

John of Karpathos. 1979. "Texts for the Monks in India." In *The Philokalia: The Complete Text*, vol. 1, compiled by Nikodimos of the Holy Mountain and Macarius of Corinth. Translated and edited by G. H. E. Palmer, Philip Sherrard, and Kallistos Ware. London: Faber.

May, Gerald. 1988. *Addiction and Grace*. San Francisco: Harper and Row.

Miller, Sue. 1999. *While I Was Gone*. New York: Ballantine.

Miller, Alice. 1985. *For Your Own Good: Hidden Cruelty in Child-Rearing and the Roots of Violence*. 2nd ed. Translated by Hildegarde and Hunter Hannum. New York: Farrar, Straus, Giroux.

O'Reilley, Mary Rose. 1993. *The Peaceable Classroom*. Portsmouth, NH: Boynton/Cook.

———. 2001. *The Barn at the End of the World: The Apprenticeship of a Quaker, Buddhist Shepherd*. Minneapolis, MN: Milkweed Editions.

Palmer, Parker. 2004. *A Hidden Wholeness*: The Journey Toward an Undivided Life. San Francisco: Jossey-Bass.

Penington, Isaac. n.d. *The Light Within and Selected Writings of Isaac Penington*. Philadelphia, PA: The Tract Association of Friends.

Pye, David. 1995. *The Nature and Art of Workmanship*. Cambium Press.

Rilke, Rainier Maria. 1984. *Letters to a Young Poet*. Translated by Stephen Mitchell. New York: Vintage Books, Random House.

———. 1989. "An Archaic Torso of Apollo." In *The Selected Poetry of Rainier Maria Rilke*. Edited and translated by Stephen Mitchell. New York: Vintage Books, Random House.

Rumi, Jalal al-Din. 2001. *The Soul of Rumi*. Translated by Coleman Barks. San Francisco: HarperSanFrancisco.

Soelle, Dorothee. 1977. *Revolutionary Patience*. Maryknoll, NY: Orbis.

———. 1984. *The Strength of the Weak: Toward a Christian Feminist Identity*. Translated by Robert and Rita Kimber. Philadelphia, PA: Westminster.

Suzuki, Shunryo. 1973. *Zen Mind, Beginner's Mind*. New York: Weatherhill.

Thoreau, Henry David. 1986. *Walden and Civil Disobedience*. New York: Penguin.

Vonnegut, Kurt. 1974. "Address to the Graduating Class at Bennington College, 1970." In *Wampeters, Foma and Granfalloons*. New York: Dell.

Weil, Simone. 1977. "Spiritual Autobiography." In *The Simone Weil Reader*. Edited by George A. Panichas. New York: David McKay.

Wolff-Salin, Mary. 1988. *The Shadow Side of Community and the Growth of Self*. New York: Crossroad.

Woolf, Virginia. 1992. *Jacob's Room*. London: Penguin.